Sir Leslie Stephen's

MAUSOLEUM BOOK

Sir Leslie Stephen

Sir Leslie Stephen's
MAUSOLEUM BOOK

With an Introduction
BY
ALAN BELL

CLARENDON PRESS · OXFORD
1977

Oxford University Press, Walton Street, Oxford OX2 6DP

OXFORD LONDON GLASGOW NEW YORK
TORONTO MELBOURNE WELLINGTON CAPE TOWN
IBADAN NAIROBI DAR ES SALAAM LUSAKA ADDIS ABABA
KUALA LUMPUR SINGAPORE JAKARTA HONG KONG TOKYO
DELHI BOMBAY CALCUTTA MADRAS KARACHI

British Library Cataloguing in Publication Data
Stephen, *Sir* Leslie
  The mausoleum book.
  1. Stephen, *Sir* Leslie
  I. Title
  820'.9   PR5473.S6

ISBN 0-19-812084-2

Printed in Great Britain by
Cox & Wyman Ltd, London, Fakenham, Reading

PREFACE

THE large green album prominently lettered PRIVATE in which Leslie Stephen inscribed a long autobiographical letter to his second wife's children (George, Stella and Gerald Duckworth; Vanessa, Thoby, Virginia and Adrian Stephen) remained in family hands—for most of the time in Vanessa Bell's studio— until Spring 1973, when it was sold to the British Museum for the benefit of the London Library. It is now Additional Manuscript 57920 in the British Library. As Stephen himself had hoped, it was used (with great circumspection) by F. W. Maitland when writing his friend's biography published in 1906, and other passages are quoted in Noël Annan's study of *Leslie Stephen* (1951): otherwise it remained unseen outside the family. Quentin Bell, who used it when preparing the first volume of his *Virginia Woolf* (1972), had previously written about it in *A Review of English Literature* VI(1965), pp. 9–18. It is now published complete for the first time.

I am indebted to the proprietors of copyright, Professor Quentin Bell, Mrs. Angelica Garnett, Mrs. Ian Parsons, Mrs. Ann Synge and Mr. Nigel Henderson, for giving me permission to publish it, and particularly to Quentin Bell for his encouragement and wise advice. I acknowledge the permission of the British Library Board for allowing me to publish their manuscript, and that of the Librarian of the Houghton Library, Harvard University, and of the Curator of the Henry W. and Albert A. Berg Collection, New York Public Library, to quote from manuscript letters in my Introduction. I am much indebted to Nicolas Barker, John Gross and Daniel Waley for their encouragement at an early stage, and I have also to thank Professor C. Richard Sanders. Hilary Bennison and Christina Sharp coped very efficiently with the typing, and my wife has given me prolonged help in checking the text: I am very grateful to them all.

Edinburgh   ALAN BELL
January 1977

CONTENTS

LIST OF ILLUSTRATIONS

THE FRONTISPIECE IS FROM THE FINAL PLATE OF F. W. MAITLAND'S *The Life and Letters of Leslie Stephen*, 1906. THE REMAINING ILLUSTRATIONS COME FROM STEPHEN'S OWN ALBUM (IN A BINDING SIMILAR TO THE 'MAUSOLEUM BOOK' MANUSCRIPT), NOW OWNED BY PROFESSOR AND MRS. QUENTIN BELL, BY WHOSE KIND PERMISSION THEY ARE REPRODUCED.

INTRODUCTION

LITTLE more than a fortnight after he was bereaved of his second wife, Leslie Stephen sought to assuage his terrible grief by writing the intimate history of his marriages. He brought to the task the literary accomplishments of a celebrated practitioner of the higher journalism, the factual objectivity of a skilled biographical editor, and the emotional power of an intricate, fascinating and usually concealed personality. Each of these qualities is amply demonstrated in the memoir which resulted from his intense efforts, the volume which became known in his family as the 'Mausoleum Book' (and which will be so called here). In spite of his intentions, what was meant to be a domestic, epistolary document became a work of literature, almost by accident taking on the appearance more of a book than a letter. Form, style and balance reveal the professional man of letters throughout and, although a number of extracts have been published previously in biographies, the shape of the *Mausoleum Book* and most of its contents are now displayed for the first time. The method of composition—careful documentary research is revealed in the drafting, where there is a particular stress on the exact identification of persons and dates —shows the editor of the *Dictionary of National Biography* at work on a composition for which a less meticulous approach would have been pardonable. (Because of this obvious care in presentation, no footnotes have been intruded into the text; the index takes in such additional information as is necessary.) As for the spiritual emphasis of a work written at the height of grief and love, the purgative and therapeutic effects of its preparation are best shown in a letter which Leslie Stephen wrote to his Harvard friend, Charles Eliot Norton, on 28 June 1895:

I will not dwell on feelings which you, if any one, understand. I am well in bodily health—only with a sense of utter exhaustion and want of interest in every outside thing. I shall, I hope, recover strength and get enough courage to face the few remaining years. But—I will say one thing. I have passed these fearful weeks partly in putting together old letters and in writing a little document for the exclusive benefit of her children. I could do nothing else; but it has interested me and made me feel nearer to her and, I hope, stamped upon me certain impressions which are now my most valuable possession. I want the children to know what the impressions were and I think that I shall leave them a little treasure to be read by themselves when I have become a memory too.

The work has brought out certain things in a manner almost painfully vivid. It has shown me her character or rather made my knowledge of it more living than ever. It has showed me what I have lost. It has, too, made real and living for me the memory of what I may call the pathetic romance of my life. Of the year before our marriage, when her pity slowly became a love such as few women indeed are capable of and she gradually decided to take up life again after having been half-dead for years, I should like to tell you the story myself as far as it is fitting to be told . . . My own part in the story was commonplace enough. *She* showed a nobility of character such as I regarded then, I am glad to say, and always since with reverence—it is the only word though it hardly expresses all. Yet it gives me this comfort, too, that I feel that whatever faults I had and however many troubles I incidentally caused, I loved her from first to last with my whole soul and that she knew it. In the hideous morbid dreams which came to me, I could not escape from self-reproaches— perhaps not all unjust—that I had not made my love clearer. And yet I know now, and these letters have made me believe it, that with all my faults, I at least worshipped her. She was the most beautiful woman I ever saw; and the beauty was her—her soul and character—as well as the outward form. I wish that I had been worthier but I *was* devoted absolutely.[1]

Denied the traditional Christian consolations by a conviction strong enough to allow the free use of words like 'reverence' and 'worship', Stephen derived much strength and comfort from the compilation of his story. The result may be emotionally self-indulgent, but it is for that reason emotionally self-revealing in a way which makes the *Mausoleum Book* an exceptional—perhaps a unique—study of late Victorian grief (and of agnostic grief, too). Specious or disingenuous much of the apologetic self-analysis may appear, particularly when the distressing domestic surroundings and attitudes of his last years are taken into account, but a tendency to self-disparagement in his literary as well as in his intimate life had long been a characteristic attitude; in setting it down so fully he was running entirely true to form. Stephen brought to the not unpleasurable literary duty of the mourner the methodical approach of the scholar. Accompanying the main *Mausoleum Book* in the British Library are a heavily-revised draft and a 'calendar of correspondence' which work out the chronological framework and to some extent prefigure the emotional structure of the autobiographical narrative. The quarto volume of 'calendar' runs to 157 pages in Stephen's small handwriting, and begins 'I am going to try to make a calendar of my correspondence which same day my children may read if they please. It is chiefly meant to refresh my own memory. I begin with the letters to and from Minny which are in the wooden box on my study mantelpiece.'[2] The resulting calendar of letters to and from both wives is informed by an odd mixture of meticulous dating (with calculations from golden numbers showing his concern for exactitude) and sentimental recollection prompted by the re-examined correspondence: 'Dear little letters, all that are left from that delightful time! . . . Nobody alas can remember but me and my memory is faint already. It will be a blank pretty soon' (p. 7). Here and elsewhere his manner is ruminatively conversational: 'From my letters of [1875] it appears that I went with Wolstenholme to Wastdale (probably at Easter) which I had quite forgotten' (p. 29). This gradually builds up into passages which form the basis of the running commentary in the *Mausoleum Book* itself:

And now [he wrote on 26 June 1895] I have read through all my Minny's letters to me and mine to her. They have given me some moments of happiness—even in my misery. Partly as I read, I went back to the past; and partly, the past is remote enough to have become a part of the inevitable. The desire to alter has been killed by the lapse of time. I can read as I could a story of imagination about the happiness of long dead people in byegone centuries. The letters, however, will lose their meaning when I am dead; nor could any living person, except possibly Anny, read in them even now what I read. I read her sweet simplicity, her childlike humour, her intense love of Anny and Laura and me and her delight in my mother . . . It

is all gone and I shall go soon. I don't know what my children will
think, if ever they look at this: but they ought to think one thing, that
I was the most fortunate of men to have the love of two such women
in succession. Whether I 'deserved' it or precisely what is meant by
deserving it, matters little. I deserved it, if love could deserve it. And I
would not have purchased freedom even from the cruel pangs that
have followed my losses by even an infinitesimal diminution of the
love that made my life beautiful.[3]

This reflection, provoked by the documents of a love long past
but still throwing an aura of grateful reminiscence over the
miseries of a newly-shattered and even more intense second
love, sets the tone for the treatment of Stephen's correspondence
with Julia Duckworth which occupies the greater part of the
'calendar' and forms the central portion of the *Book*.

The original letters of his second courtship and marriage
have survived and are available in the Berg Collection of New
York Public Library. They make astonishing reading, in
physical quantity and in intensity of feeling, even after the
prolonged tensions and anxieties chronicled in the *Mausoleum
Book* are understood. They contain much incidental biographical information to supplement both this memoir and our
knowledge of Stephen's world, but what is really remarkable
is the controlled and artistic use which Stephen was able to
make of documents pulsating with an emotion which stood
little chance of being recollected in tranquillity. The literary
ordering of a year's correspondence in which a forceful passion,
neither unrestrained nor undignified, reflects the intellectual
and probably the sexual tension of the principal writer and
suffuses even the day-to-day recitation of domestic details,
would be a difficult task for any biographer. For the task to
have been carried out so skilfully by a newly-bereaved auto-
biographer indicates a degree of intellectual control which
must be weighed against the unrestrained lamentation which
is one of the main features of the *Mausoleum Book*.

The process of compilation started in the 'calendar' was
continued in the draft which survives alongside the principal
text (as Add.MS.57921). This is clearly but speedily written,
full (for Stephen) of ink alterations made *currente calamo*, with
ink addenda in a smaller and shakier hand on the facing
versos. The whole has been revised in pencil, this writing being

tremulous to the point of illegibility. Stephen himself noted on
19 July (having commenced the volume on 21 May) that
'I copied this out and mean to have the copy bound in a volume
with some photographs, etc. [This was never done.] The copy is
a good deal altered especially in the later part and is the more
authentic version, as I corrected my impressions by rereading
letters, etc.'[4] The alterations are nearly always improvements,
and the addenda on the draft, which develop significant
incidents or character portrayals, increase the impression of
literary craftsmanship. The 'letter to Julia's children' can be
seen to have achieved in draft the consistency of emotional
force which makes it so memorable a document; the work of
transcribing it into the large green morocco album (which
occupied Stephen between 4 and 11 July 1895) added little,
emotionally, to the intense feelings derived from his intimate
archives in May. The text of the *Mausoleum Book* is therefore
given below as Stephen left it, with minor adjustments of
spelling, punctuation, and presentation (the author, a notori-
ously bad proof-reader, was far from careful of these matters),
but with the distracting cross-references to the volume of
Extracts (as he called the 'calendar') removed.[5] Minor errors
of transcription discovered between his *Mausoleum Book* texts
and those in the 'calendar' or the original letters have been left
unremarked; this is intended to be a simple presentation of the
Book, not an edition of correspondence which deserves detailed
treatment separately.

The *Mausoleum Book* proper was the vehicle for various
memoranda (such as the note of Huxley's funeral on p. 8), but
Stephen left the text alone, reserving the later pages of the
volume for 'a few notes . . . of anything likely to interest you
hereafter'. The mixture of family chronicle and occasional
obituary record which follows is more akin to Stephen's
activities as biographer-cum-autobiographer, which longevity
over his circle had made an important part of the literary work
of his later years. Articles for periodicals or the *Dictionary of
National Biography*, or introductions to collections of essays, on
men like James Payn, George Smith, Henry Sidgwick and
James Dykes Campbell, have their briefer counterpart in the
second section of the *Mausoleum Book*. There were earlier
works, too, which show that he was becoming skilled in

reminiscent biography. He wrote lives of Henry Fawcett (1885) and of his brother Sir James Fitzjames Stephen (1895), both of which owe their standing not to their unexpected command of governmental or legal technicalities but to the element of autobiography which they contain. The really striking passages of *Fawcett* deal with their shared Cambridge years, and the common family upbringing gives a penetrating quality to the earlier chapters of the *Stephen*, where the evangelical background is handled incisively but with a welcome lightness of touch. As well as providing an opportunity for Stephen to abridge the *Mausoleum Book* (references are several times made to these biographies), they show that the autobiographical mode was never far from his call in literature, as well as being a very characteristic habit of mind in life. The form and manner of the strictly autobiographical portions of the *Mausoleum Book* came to him frequently and naturally; the later essays, 'Some Early Impressions', published in the *National Review* of 1903 (and by the Hogarth Press in 1924) are a disappointingly weak, mannered and discursive specimen.

Another autobiographical work which is referred to in the *Mausoleum Book* is less easy to assess. 'Forgotten Benefactors' is the last essay in *Social Rights and Duties*, the two volumes of Stephen's addresses to Ethical Societies published in 1896. Much of the address is devoted to the unremembered services of the least of men in human history, discussed in a manner rather better suited to the study than to the platform. Few examples are adduced, but there is yet another reference to Thomas Hughes's brother who 'somehow represented with singular completeness a beautiful moral type'.[6] A passage on the domestic influence of womankind is supported by a further quoting of Wordsworth's 'a perfect woman, nobly planned . . .', which (like so much of Wordsworth) was such a comfort to him in successive widowerhoods. Then the essay turns to Stephen's personal experience and to recent events of which his hearers would have been well aware. As in the *Mausoleum Book* he spoke (but here anonymously) of Julia's nobility of nature having been

struck by one of those terrible blows which shiver the very foundations of life; which make the outside world a mere discordant nightmare, and seem to leave for the only reality a perpetual and gnawing pain, which lulls for an instant only to be revived by every contact with facts . . . Yet the greatest test of true nobility of character is its power of turning even the bitterest grief to account . . . by slow degrees it undergoes a transmutation into more steady and profound love of whatsoever may still be left.[7]

Such a nature 'acquires claims not only upon our love but on our reverence'. Stephen's awareness of his own inability to respond nobly to such a challenge increased his reverence the more. Generalizing from his own grief seems to have strained him stylistically, and 'Forgotten Benefactors' lacks the literary control of the *Mausoleum Book*. The strain was perhaps religious as well as literary: in spite of his determined agnosticism, could there perhaps have been some hankering after the consolations which the discarded religion might have offered? The *Mausoleum Book* (as we shall see) and the correspondence on which it is based make references to Julia's sainthood. This is the conventional canonization of an intense courtship, but when the notion is displayed in a sermon to an Ethical gathering the effect is somewhat different:

But that man is unfortunate who has not a saint of his own—some one in whose presence, or in the very thought of whom, he does not recognize a superior, before whom it becomes him to bow with reverence and gratitude, and who has purified the atmosphere and strengthened the affections in a little circle from which the influence may be transmitted to others. The saint will be forgotten all too soon— long before less valuable, but accidentally more conspicuous, services have passed out of mind—but the moral elevation, even of a small circle, is a benefit which may be propagated indefinitely.[8]

Like lentils dressed as meat at the vegetarian table, these musings before an Ethical congregation have about them an aura of conventional religiosity, not least in their attempted replacement of an after-life by a continuing immanence of memory:

We may yet learn to feel as if those who left us had yet become part of ourselves; that we have become so permeated by their influence, that we can still think of their approval and sympathy as a stimulating and elevating power, and be conscious that we are more or less carrying on their work, in their spirit.[9]

Little of this finds its way into the *Mausoleum Book*, where the force of the deceased's character and the strength of familiar memory made such feelings self-evident. The tenor of the agnostic statement does not indicate any real, religious, doubt, for to Stephen a simple and binding decision had been made long before. He could not however bring himself to state the matter as firmly as Norton did in a letter of 1892, soon after Stephen had lost his mother-in-law:

People talk of the consolations of religion, but they seem generally to be delusive. You and I, I believe, who have given them up, stand really upon firmer ground for the meeting of sorrow. To accept the irremediable for what it really is, not trying to deceive one's self about it, or to elude it, or to put it into a fancy dress, is to secure simple relations with life, and tends to strengthen the character without, I trust, any hardening of heart or narrowing of sympathies. It should save from cynicism and bitterness of temper.[10]

Norton, a kindred spirit, offered after Julia's death the consolation that 'there is still something to be done in life', although he added

But one has to learn to live without joy, and without the hope of it. The hardest time is, perhaps, yet to come, when the excitement of immediate sorrow and the need of constant strenuous effort is past; when the dreary routine of the joyless days begins, and when the sense of solitude and diminished personality weighs heavier and heavier. The death of her whom one has truly loved is the end of the best of one's-self.[11]

That prognostication was too readily appreciated by Leslie Stephen to make it easy for him to offer any simple comforts in his sermon.

The faith which he had put away is as little discussed in the *Mausoleum Book* as in his other writings. He regarded the questions which had influenced him in disavowing his profession of faith, matters of the authenticity of the Flood, or of Joshua and the Amorites, as 'commonplace and prosaic', but at least he does not dispose of them for the family with the glibness he displayed in *Some Early Impressions* (where 'exchange the pulpit for the press', 'I had given up Noah's Ark and my old calling' come too pat).[12] His increasing conviction 'that Noah's

flood was a fiction (or rather that I had never believed in it)'—
the use of the word *believe* raising nice ontological considerations
—must be set in the *Zeitgeist* (as Noël Annan has done admirably
in his *Leslie Stephen: his thought and character in relation to his time*
of 1951), but the sincerity and simplicity of the rejection
cannot be denied. In 1901 Stephen wrote to William James,
who was preparing the Gifford Lectures which became *The
Varieties of Religious Experience*:

You ask me to give my own religious experience, to which I can only
say that if you could cross-examine me viva voce you might possibly
attract some ideas. But left to myself I can say no more than 'Story,
God bless you, I have none to tell'. I seem to myself to have had no
spiritual history whatever, except that I gradually shed some old
formulae and did not regret them because I had never much believed
in them. It is all too painfully commonplace to supply even a sentence
—not a paragraph— in a lecture. And now I find myself becoming
more commonplace than ever.[13]

Stephen's nature, withdrawn, shy and prickly though it
seemed to outsiders and even to some of his closest circle of
male friends who usually knew better, was on an intimate level
simply passionate, impulsive, demanding of the giving and
receiving of a devotion which might help to replace those of the
religious forms which he had rejected. One object of devotion
was the Alps; Douglas Freshfield said with justice that 'the
Alps were for Stephen a playground, but they were also a
cathedral'.[14] The real filling of the need was not in moun-
taineering but in marriage. The Alps became a holy place
largely because of their close connection with the 'saints' he
married. Of the first, Minny Thackeray, what he writes in the
Mausoleum Book, skilfully using contrasts with her surviving
sister to convey a personality to the next generation, is probably
as much as we are likely to know. As so little correspondence is
available to document the marriage, one can only see it as a
conventional happy wedlock, easing him (but only a little way)
out of the donnish shell of which he was too well aware by an
infusion of those Thackeray spirits which Anny had in even
ampler measure than Minny. The elements of Leslie's devotion
were there, but they were not yet fully developed. Of the first
wife, Leslie's sister was later to write

She had a singular and indescribable social charm—a humorous, wayward and changeful grace, which captivated not only for the moment but for life, because its freshness was so unmistakeably the outcome of transparent sincerity. She was, beyond any one I have ever known, quaintly picturesque, tender and true. She could never have been put into intellectual harness, but there was a rare sureness and delicacy in her critical intuitions, whether as to personal or literary qualities. Her own pen, though sparingly used, had a felicity worthy of her parentage. But what comes back most vividly in one's memory of her is the native half playful motherliness of her household ways, which was both amusing and pathetic in the youngest and most fragile of the little family party. It is good to remember that for the last five years of her life she tasted the purest delight of motherhood through her own child. Altogether the eight years of their married life was a spring-time of beauty and gladness for both.[15]

Fortunately she was spared the gradual recognition of their daughter's mental incapacity, which is frequently referred to in the *Mausoleum Book* and in his more intimate correspondence, and which was to form a bond between Stephen and Mrs. Julia Duckworth.

The sudden rupture of the marriage by Minny's death on 28 November 1875, and the grief which followed, refined and intensified Stephen's need for an object of marital devotion, and the core of the *Book* shows how it was satisfied. Noël Annan has written of the second marriage:

His love for Minny had been protective, jocular, cossetting. In Julia he recognized a deeper and more sensitive character than his own and one who had borne sorrow, as he would have wished to bear it, but could not. He worshipped her with unalterable devotion— 'Good God, how that man adores her', said Henry James . . . Indeed, worship was what he sought in marriage; a living image before whom he could pour out the flood of devotion that could find no outlet in religion. He idealised her and longed to sacrifice himself for her— which in the day-to-day routine of home life he was quite incapable of doing.[16]

Julia Stephen, in spite of all that is written in the *Mausoleum Book,* and perhaps even because of the various accounts in her daughter Virginia's writings, will always remain a rather elusive, enigmatic figure; in some measure this is because (as Quentin Bell has put it) 'Leslie Stephen has drawn the portrait of a saint and because she is a saint one cannot quite believe in her'.[17] We know more of the marriage, even if the bride eludes us. The domestic circumstances of both parties scarcely permitted a renewal of the relatively high spirits of Stephen's first marriage. ('I don't care to be in high spirits,' he wrote to Norton in 1878, 'but I feel a very delightful sense of calm and contented acceptance of what may come.')[18] But the mood was far from sombre and the reverential tone never filled them with gloom, particularly after their own children arrived to demonstrate that domestic contentment was not irretrievable.

The highly devotional tone of Stephen's declaration of love in courtship and in widowhood is of course at odds with the realities of his married life. The *Mausoleum* is not only a stately burial place erected by Stephen for a person of distinction, and one in which he could indulge his sentimental feelings for the honorand. It also provides a vehicle for the moods of self-recrimination which came to him so frequently, for rehearsing the petty (or not so petty) disputes with Anny over money and other matters, and the demands—emotional and physical— which he made on Julia. He was all too well aware that of the many burdens which she took upon herself, the emotional custody of her hypersensitive and appallingly honest spouse was by far the heaviest. 'He worshipped Julia', Noël Annan has written, and:

desired to transform her into an apotheosis of motherhood, but treated her in the home as someone who should be at his beck and call, support him in every emotional crisis, order the minutiae of his life and then submit to his criticism in those household matters of which she was mistress.[19]

Declarations of unreasonable domestic and emotional exigence pepper the marital correspondence as well as this memoir, but the demands he made of her were none the less importunate for being so openly confessed. A letter avowedly written to 'coax a little sympathy' was none the less troublesome to a dutifully sympathetic wife for being prefaced by so disingenuously honest a declaration. 'Although there were matters', Virginia Stephen wrote in a family memoir designed for her nephew, 'which seem to us now decided by her too much in a spirit of compromise, and exacted by him without strict regard for justice or magnanimity, still it is true whether you judge by their work or by themselves that [Julia's] was a triumphant life, consistently aiming at higher things.'[20] The whole tension of the marriage between the exalted ideal and the temperamentally demanding day-to-day reality may be judged from the tone of self-recrimination in the *Mausoleum Book* and the realization (based on our knowledge of Stephen's later years) that there was indeed much of which he might justifiably accuse himself.

Stephen was much less fair to himself when assessing his own literary career. Self-depreciatory comments are frequent in the *Mausoleum Book*, but it was his recurrent habit of mind to place himself unjustly low in the scale of intellectual achievement, both personally (with a feeling of having 'scattered' himself too much) or in relation to his times (with a sense, appropriate to a *Dictionary* editor, of belonging to the footnotes rather than to the main text of intellectual history). As Maitland put it in a caveat introducing some of the autobiographical extracts, 'behind the irony and the humour and the artistic self-effacement there was unaffected modesty: an estimate of his own powers and achievements which, if it seemed to some of us absurdly low, was none the less unquestionably genuine'.[21] In the context of the *Mausoleum Book* these self-doubtings may seem to be the maudlin thoughts of one disorientated by death, but they had a much longer history. The period of mental and physical exhaustion produced by his strenuous work on the *Dictionary* had also been a time of self-depreciation from which not even his wife's energetic remonstrances could budge him:

I wonder why it is: but when I am by myself I always begin thinking what poor stuff all my writing is. It does not make me angry nor depressed: but I see that as a fact I have done enough in the author way to show that I could have done something decent if I had not wasted myself. That is my serious conviction and probably the only absurdity is in thinking about the possibility that I might have done more—which is one variety of vanity. Does this make you angry? I don't know why I should say it, if it does: but it occurs to me and I may as well speak my mind. The practical moral is that I may as well do dictionary as anything else.[22]

In the following Spring such feelings, which had been induced largely by overwork ('moral,' he wrote to Norton on running

the Clark lectureship in harness with the *Dictionary*, 'it is a
mistake to take work for one's left hand while the right is full')[23]
seem to have been dispersed. 'Dictionary and other bothers are
really very superficial,' he wrote to Julia, 'they ruffle my temper
but they don't disturb me below the surface much. I am solidly
happy especially so long as the little ones are tolerably well.'[24]
He probably became too revolted by the incubus of the
Dictionary and too justly appreciative of Lee's work as assistant
and then as editor to assess fairly his own part in its planning
and execution. The *Mausoleum Book* records his feelings about
it, and there is plenty of supporting correspondence (which I
hope to give fuller treatment elsewhere). Yet along with the
impression of toil which they give, there is from an early stage a
consciousness of working well for posterity. 'It is hard work', he
had written to Julia in January 1883, 'but not altogether
uninteresting and it is pleasant to be employed on a really
solid job. If well done, it will be a valuable thing for generations,
even for To's [Thoby's] grandchildren.'[25]

It is a pity that the toil of *Dictionary* work later prevented his
maintaining this optimistic mood, for it has indeed proved to
be the most enduring brass of his monument. His achievement
as it is now generally recognized would have surprised him,
and must be contrasted with the nakedly honest but misleading
self-assessment of the *Mausoleum Book*, whose remarks go
deeper than the coat-trailing and fishing for compliments to
which Julia was sometimes subjected. The ethical and original
philosophical writings on which he set so high a value have
long been held at a discount, but his work as editor, biographer,
historian of ideas, alpinist, and perhaps above all as a literary
critic of an admirable temper of mind, is far from being
consigned to the oblivion which he in his self-deceiving honesty
felt it deserved.[26]

The literary side of Stephen's autobiography has naturally
been sacrificed to the personal, and one can only regret that
he chose to say so little about his literary friends outside his
family circle. His remark 'I pass by [Lewes, Trollope, Huxley,
Spencer and others], telling you nothing of them and, indeed,
having little to tell' is, however, characteristic.[27] Occasional
astringent *obiter dicta* (as, for example, on George Eliot) seem
promising, but few even of his general family letters contain

the telling anecdotes which he would have been so well placed
to record had his cast of mind, and indeed the bias of his
memory, lain in that direction: the essays in *Some Early
Impressions* are likewise sparse in literary recollection.
Tennyson is sometimes referred to in the letters, in domestic
surroundings, and Ruskin (with whom Stephen had a prolonged
and uneasy relationship) comes into the story of the courtship
of Julia when so many letters were written from Coniston in
1877. But in the letters as in the *Mausoleum Book* such eminent
contemporaries are brought in only because of their place in the
family history. The acerbities which Stephen inserted about
Henry Halford Vaughan are the most prominent example.
They are specially interesting because Vaughan's example led
Stephen, with Carlyle also in mind, to reflect upon his own
marriage. Stephen's attitude to Vaughan was firm even in
1881–5, and letters of that period show that his judgement of the
marriage, and his view that Mrs. Vaughan's devotion was
misplaced, were contemporaneous with the events described.
The sourly amusing literary assessment, which one might have
thought had been elaborated in recollection, was also firmly
established by 1885, as Stephen made clear to Norton while
examining the pitiable literary remains of the failed philosopher:

So far as I have gone, they are a chaos, and, unluckily, I fear that if
they could be arranged they would be worthless. They are beginnings
of speculations—of a kind antiquated by more modern books which
he never read—about some sort of philosophical theory which never
gets out of preliminary apparatus and logical prolegomena. It is
melancholy to plunge into all this mass, representing merely the waste
of what must once have been a fine intellect. Piles on piles of—nothing.
Poor man, I fancy something was wrong in his brain latterly and the
whole thing might be put in the fire tomorrow without loss to any
one. However I am too busy to have sounded it all as yet, and there
may be older and better bits in this monstrous mass—not that I expect
it.[28]

The passages on Stephen's sister-in-law Anny Thackeray
Ritchie also blend literary and family comment. Even though
Anny is used as a mirror in which something of Minny's
personality might dimly be perceived, the pages devoted to
her are written with a far from ill-humoured edge and provide
some light relief from the more sombre mood of the rest of the

memoir. In the draft one can see how the whole digression on Anny was reworked until pace, and more particularly *tone*, were artistically settled; literary and personal criticisms were carefully balanced. The incident of Stephen's discovering Richmond Ritchie embracing his godmother and (even at that stage) wife-to-be has also been worked up into a smooth narrative. Yet such literary revisions should not be taken as showing a re-thought and malicious approach to that forceful and agreeable, but (particularly to a reclusive scholar) infinitely maddening character. In March 1876 he wrote to Norton reflecting on his recent loss of Minny, remarking that 'Anny Thackeray is little short of the angels. She has real genius so far as genius can be made out of affection and sympathy. She sympathizes indeed so quickly that people who don't know her sometimes doubt her perfect sincerity. The doubt is a complete mistake.'[29] Stephen's frustrated appreciation of his sister-in-law comes out in the letters to Julia, frankly expressed and (as he admitted) sometimes overstated. A long discussion of female education at a time when the tutoring of Laura was still being considered contains a passage on Anny:

You speak as if I were a schoolmaster like Cornish who valued people by the place they could take in a tripos. Nothing could be less like my views. Education is a very good thing, and so are good clothes; but I like people for what they are, not for what they have got. Anny, for example, is about the most uneducated person I ever knew. She has not two facts in her head and one of them is a mistake. But certainly I think her one of the best and most attractive people I ever met—and worth a dozen senior wranglers and the whole staff of professors at Girton and Newnham. What I said of her want of education is what I should say (I suppose) of a first-rate musical performer who had a bad violin. His talent might be first rate but I imagine that his music would be spoilt for most people. Anny always reminds me of an admirable painter whose colours or brushes or something or other are so confused that all her outlines are muddled and indistinct. She would not lose her genius nor have more genius if she were as clever in her workmanship as Miss Austen; but she would be incomparably more successful.[30]

There was something about Anny which called for lavish metaphor to express it. Stephen never found it easy to convey his feelings about his sister-in-law and her work, the obvious resemblance to Minny making it all the more difficult. Julia protested at the tone of the extract quoted and received in reply the comment that

I am sorry if I vexed you; but you know that Anny's writings never were quite appreciable by me. I suppose that we agree in thinking her better than her books. Still I know that I am not quite just to her writing. Certain superficial defects irritate my methodical editorial mind; for I feel how often the 'general reader' must be at a loss to know what she is driving at. But she has real genius and originality— more than almost anybody now working—if only it could be just a little combed out![31]

The same ambivalent approach, compounded of affection and annoyance, is to be found in the *Mausoleum Book* twenty years later. There is little affection displayed either in the correspondence or the memoir in their account of Anny's courtship and marriage—disgust at the disparity in age, apprehension by Stephen of his awkward domestic predicament, made him bitter in a way which showed throughout his life. The general opinion had been surprised but favourable. George Eliot wrote to Mme Bodichon that 'the nearly 20 years' difference between them was bridged hopefully by his solidarity and gravity. This is one of several instances that I have known of lately, showing that young men with even brilliant advantages will often choose as their life's companion a woman whose attractions are wholly of the spiritual order.'[32] Mrs. Jebb wrote that 'everybody considers him fortunate in spite of the difference in age. Her charm depends not at all upon either youth or beauty and is very universally felt. He will be sure to be proud of her, and is himself so silent and so peculiar that he looks even ten years older than he is.'[33]

Leslie Stephen could not of course have seen the impending marriage in so favourable a light. 'You tell me next', he wrote to Julia, 'that R[ichmond] is in a state of rapture—Let him! I am glad that I am not there to see. I am always afraid of having a scrimmage some day with A[nny] in his company; whereupon he would interfere; whereupon a scene would occur: a general blow-up, tears, reconciliation and all the rest of it. However there is no danger for the present.' And a couple of days later, by way of apology for this outburst he wrote that

Richmond, my dear, *will* come between me and Anny more than you
know or think. It will not be her fault: but mine . . . I shall certainly
drift further away—it is no use denying it. I would do anything in
the world for her, but I cannot and shall not feel close to her after she
has taken up with that boy. All this sounds rather brutal, but there is a
painful degree of truth in it.[34]

'The mixture of painful feeling comes possibly in fact from
the kind of unreasonable jealousy which, I suppose, fathers feel
for sons-in-law; and which one can only endeavour to expel by
degrees.'[35] Although Stephen could explain his attitude, he
could neither dissemble nor overcome it; nor, as we shall see,
could he learn from experience when an actual (step) son-in-
law came into his life. Most of his rows with Anny had been
short and sharp: 'A. and I never had a quarrel which lasted
from luncheon to dinner. There was never any malice in them
and there could not be. She was much too candid and I was
never afraid of any ill feeling in the background.'[36] The Richmond Ritchie business was different in quality, and led to
estrangement. Anny remained buoyantly on visiting terms,
however, and was a frequent visitor in Stephen's last years,
when she was never repelled by 'the jeremiads and invectives
he poured into her sympathetic ear'. 'Well Leslie,' she once
said on entering, to anticipate and dispel the inevitable recitation of misery, 'Damn—Damn—DAMN!'[37]

The account of his stepdaughter Stella Duckworth's courtship, marriage and brutally sudden death in the second part of
the *Mausoleum Book* is all too brief. As well as offering some
interesting parallels with the Anny affair it takes us deeply
into Stephen's relationship with the next generation. We know
enough of Stella's life and death from Virginia's autobiographical writings and other documents to see that what
Stephen wrote for the family is misleading. The close similarities
of temperament between Stella and her mother, both of them
beautiful, devoted and submissive, made it all too easy for her
to fall into the role of surrogate wife as far as Stephen's heavy
emotional demands were concerned. We can see in his attitude
to the engagement and wedding something of the jealousy
and feeling of being threatened domestically which had
manifested itself so strongly before Anny's marriage. More
importantly, the force of the emotional pressure to which

Stella was exposed is an indication of the similar demands Stephen must have made on his wife. Jack Hills's prolonged and persistent courtship had long been encouraged by Julia, even more assiduous as a matchmaker here than in other recorded negotiations. The long courtship gave Stephen plenty of time for self-pitying forebodings. He wrote to Norton in 1895 that

Stella is my great support now; she is very like her mother in some ways—very sweet and noble and affectionate to me. I am sometimes worried by thinking that she ought to be a wife and mother and that she may find sufficient reasons for leaving me. I ought to wish for it and sometimes I do but from a purely selfish point of view the event would be disastrous almost for me. However I suppose that I should submit and indeed there would be compensations.[38]

The day after the engagement he wrote to Norton at some length that Julia's approval meant that he 'ought to be happy or less unhappy in consequence. I dare say that I may be when I have had time to think things over a little.' This matches the grudging delight recorded so ominously in the *Mausoleum Book* itself: 'If any thing could make me happier, this ought to, but my happiness is a matter of rapidly diminishing importance.'[39]

The new role of father-in-law was contemplated with disrelish, and on the very evening of the wedding his feelings were so intense that he felt it best to intrude them on his stepdaughter's honeymoon:

I am tired and excited and don't precisely know whether I am standing on my head or my heels. The world seems to have turned topsy-turvy with me since this morning and I feel as I felt once when I picked myself up after a fall—I cannot tell whether I am hurt or healed of a wound or simply dazzled.

Well, dearest, I am quite clear about one or two things. I know that we love each other and shall continue to love each other. I know that you will do all you can for me and that your husband will help you. I know, too, that you have done the thing which of all others, but for my selfish twist, I should have wished you to do; and that you have every chance of happiness. With all these good things to be said and said without a doubt, it seems that there must be yet something to hope for, even for me in this fag end of life. The terrible sorrow I have gone through has taught me to know you as I never knew you before and to feel that you have—what could I say more expressive?— the same nature as my darling. I said to her that I not only loved but reverenced her and I never said a truer thing. Now one cannot exactly reverence a daughter but I have the feeling which corresponds to it—you may find a name for it—but I mean that my love of you is something more than mere affection: it includes complete confidence and trust. Well, I will say no more. It is only repeating what you know. Love me still and tell me sometimes that you love me. Goodbye!⁴⁰

Stephen had rarely if ever found it necessary to write to his wife with the same intensity of feeling since he had laid epistolary siege to her emotions in 1877. It is surely possible to gauge from this letter to the young bride Stella the depth and manner of the emotional support which Stephen had over the years demanded from her mother, Julia, and which provides the unwritten reverse side of the *Mausoleum Book*'s portrait of his marriage.

The grief of the entire family at Stella's sudden death was universal and genuine. Stephen reported the tragedy to Norton, once again stressing all the similarities to Julia: 'Her help was invaluable in regard to the children, who were all on the most confidential and affectionate terms with her; and though she had left us, she seemed to be still the great bond of union in the house'. 'My Vanessa', he added, 'is taking her place as mistress of the house very calmly and will be invaluable.'⁴¹ The *Mausoleum Book* does not record this substitution and a detailed commentary on the difficulties it caused would be inappropriate here. Quentin Bell has written of the 'savage, self-pitying emotional blackmail that he inflicted on his daughters', and it is clear that the demands he made on them, particularly on Vanessa at the weekly audit of the domestic accounts, were only a symptom of his patriarchal attitude.⁴²

Against this may be set his genuine delight in his children's individuality and their achievements from an early age: this is often recorded in the second part of the *Mausoleum Book*. It shows him in a good light as a father—and as a stepfather, for he had a misplaced belief in the comradeship of the half-brothers and sisters, rejoicing indeed by 1898 that he could comfort himself 'with the thought that my children are gradually coming to the age of fuller intercourse'.⁴³ It was not only the younger generation who felt Stephen's belief in their friendship to be ill founded. Soon after Julia's death, Mrs. Jebb had written that 'I never felt quite sure of the attitude of the

Duckworth children towards the little ones, and their own step-father. I shall not be surprised if they were to part company and make two households.'[44] The domestic dispersal was not to come until 1904 and belongs to the children's biography rather than the father's. His judgement of their individual abilities was more accurate: Thoby's suitability for Cambridge was soon recognized, as was Virginia's literary potential. 'Yesterday I discussed George II with 'Ginia', he had written to his wife in 1893. 'She takes in a great deal and will really be an author in time, though I cannot make up my mind in what line. History will be a good thing for her to take up as I can give her some hints.'[45] Praise of Vanessa's drawing reported by Julia next year produced the comment 'I shall be truly glad if she has a talent that way, as I think that it will be a great pleasure for her; but she always looks to me so much like Milly that I am afraid she may turn Quaker, or whatever is the fashionable thing 20 years hence'.[46] His wholehearted encouragement of Virginia's literary and Vanessa's artistic bent does him great credit as a father. 'I cannot remember a time', Vanessa was later to write, 'when Virginia did not mean to be a writer and I a painter. It was a lucky arrangement, for it meant that we went our own ways and one source of jealousy at any rate was absent.'[47] By 1900 Stephen was able to report to Norton: 'Thoby enjoying Cambridge immoderately; and Vanessa her studio; and Virginia becoming as literary as her papa.'[48]

For Virginia in particular, the personalities and topography of her childhood were to be a rich store of reminiscence to add to her literary inheritance from the Stephens. St. Ives, recorded in the *Mausoleum Book* with affection by Stephen himself, was to be very important in Virginia's imaginative life. 'When they took Talland House, my father and mother gave me, at any rate, something I think invaluable. Suppose I had only Surrey or Sussex or the Isle of Wight to think about when I think about my childhood.'[49] It was not only the holiday house that was to be so fertile in inspiration for her. Hyde Park Gate was to be recalled for the Memoir Club in 1922:

When I look back upon that house it seems to me so crowded with scenes of family life, grotesque, comic and tragic; with the violent

emotions of youth, revolt, despair, intoxicating happiness, immense
boredom, with parties of the famous and the dull; with rages again,
George and Gerald; with love scenes with Jack Hills; with passionate
affection or my father alternating with passionate hatred of him, all
tingling and vibrating in an atmosphere of youthful bewilderment
and curiosity—that I feel suffocated by the recollection. The place
seemed tangled and matted with emotion . . . It seemed as if the house
and the family which had lived in it, thrown together as they were by
so many deaths, so many emotions, so many traditions, must endure for
ever. And then suddenly in one night both vanished.[50]

Hyde Park Gate, with all its emotional associations, continued
to be a potent intellectual and psychological influence in the
lives at least of its younger Stephen residents. Its importance in
Virginia's later life is too well known to need stressing here, and
our whole attitude to Leslie Stephen must inevitably be
coloured by the portrayal of Mr. and Mrs. Ramsay in *To the
Lighthouse* which she published in 1927. The autobiographical
element in the novel has long been seen as a reason for its
peculiar standing amongst her works. Thus F. R. Leavis wrote
in 1941 that 'the substance of the novel was provided directly
by life . . . we know enough about Leslie Stephen, the novelist's
father, and his family to know that there is a large measure of
direct transcription. We can see a clear correlation between
this fact and the unique success of *To the Lighthouse* among her
novels'.[51] This is true up to a point, although 'transcription' is
too mundane a word for the many levels of Virginia Woolf's
creative interpretation of the past; it should not in the present
documentary context mislead us into thinking of the *Mausoleum
Book* as a simple source-book for *To the Lighthouse*. Influential it
certainly was, and it is instructive to read one in the light of the
other; the edition of the *Lighthouse* manuscript which Dr. Susan
Dick has in hand will point to relevant details in the composition. It is less the indirect quotation of Stephen's text which is
important, more the 'transcription' of gestures of body and
attitudes of mind. The loosely-quoted anecdotes as well as the
portrayal of intellectual feeling owe most to an inevitable store
of family memories so strong that a direct reference to the
documents would have been superfluous.

The principal, fugal, theme of the book, on ' "Yes, of course,
if it's fine tomorrow," said Mrs. Ramsay . . . "But," said

[James's] father . . . "it won't be fine." . . . "But it may be fine —I expect it will be fine," said Mrs. Ramsay', gains when seen against Stephen's picture of himself and his marriage in the *Mausoleum Book*. The yea and nay are not antiphonal absolutes, but much more subtle, reflecting the complex attitudes of the speakers. The uncompromising intellectual integrity, the anxiety, loneliness, severity and precariously-controlled anger of Mr. Stephen/Ramsay are all there; so too are his all-important doubts of enduring literary fame (and the author's metaphor of the second-rank philosopher's only reaching Q on an alphabetical scale of intellectual achievement is surely related to Stephen's necessary concern for the literal ordering of the *Dictionary of National Biography*).[52] Yet the father in *To the Lighthouse* is never portrayed as a wholly unsympathetic character—that would have been autobiographically unjust and artistically too simple. Nor is Mrs. Stephen/Ramsay displayed merely as a white to her husband's black. To the obvious stock of proper maternal occupation and concern is added a feeling of bustling meddlesomeness, of nursery domination extended into other parts of her life—matchmaking for example— and indeed continuing after her death in a way more pervasive than her husband's for being the more subtle. The mother's view of life, fundamentally darker than the father's, is artistically valuable in avoiding too simple a contrast of mood, and this is also well shown in the *Mausoleum Book*. And in her dying as in her life the literary as well as the psychological influence is apparent. The sudden and shocking deaths of the *Mausoleum Book*—Minny's, Julia's and Stella's— are matched by Mrs. Ramsay's and Prue's deaths, reported with chilling brevity in those skilfully-employed square brackets of the entr'acte second section.

The rapid conception and the writing of *To the Lighthouse* were for Virginia Woolf a real discharge of emotion long bottled up. Obsessive recollections of her mother ceased to trouble her and she was at last able to take a balanced view of her father. 'I used to think of him and mother daily,' she wrote in her diary on what would have been his ninety-sixth birthday, 'but writing the *Lighthouse* laid them in my mind. And now he comes back sometimes, but differently . . . more as a contemporary.'[53] Four years later she was able to write of him objectively and affectionately in a short centenary article in *The Times*, an essay which is an essential counterpart to the mixed feelings displayed in *To the Lighthouse*. She writes of his physical characteristics, of his intellectual attitudes, even of his irrational worries about money—and of his enduring reputation. The praise he would most have valued, she concluded, would have been Meredith's posthumous tribute—from George Meredith, who in *The Egoist* had described his fictional image as 'Phoebus Apollo turned fasting friar'. Stephen himself had written in the *Mausoleum Book* that 'Meredith, though he has his faults, has a good heart and no man, I think, can better appreciate beauty both of the physical and moral kind'.[54] Such a discerning connoisseur of the emotions wrote to Vanessa Stephen in terms which do much to explain and justify the *Mausoleum Book*. 'He was the one man in my knowledge worthy of being mated with your mother. I could not say more of any man's nobility.'

NOTES

1. MS. Harvard. All quotations from Stephen's letters to Norton are taken from the large group in the Houghton Library, bMS Am 1088 (6880–7050), which is arranged as a chronological series.
2. British Library, Additional MS. 57922, p. 1.
3. Ibid., p. 31.
4. Add. MS. 57921, f. 1; see also p. 97 below.
5. For the excision of a superfluous chronology, see p. 97–8 below.
6. Op. cit., pp. 247–9; see also pp. 30n., 100 below.
7. *Social Rights and Duties* (1896), pp. 254–6.
8. Ibid., p. 264.
9. Ibid., p. 265.
10. Charles Eliot Norton, *Letters*, ed. Sara Norton and M. A. DeWolfe Howe (1913), II. 211.
11. Ibid., p. 228.
12. *Some Early Impressions* (1924), pp. 68, 89, 98.
13. To William James, 9 May 1901: MS. Harvard. Such a spiritual non-history enabled Stephen to take a disrespectful view of the *Varieties*, which he acknowledged with genial scepticism in July 1902.
14. F. W. Maitland, *The Life and Letters of Leslie Stephen* (1906), p. 79.
15. Ibid., p. 254.
16. N. G. Annan, *Leslie Stephen* (1951), p. 75.

17. Quentin Bell, *Virginia Woolf, A Biography*, I (1972), pp. 17–18.
18. To Norton, 4 March 1878: MS. Harvard.
19. Annan, p. 99.
20. Virginia Woolf, *Moments of Being*, ed. Jeanne Schulkind (1976),
    p. 34 (the quotation dating from 1907–8).
21. Maitland, p. 5.
22. To Julia Stephen, 4 September 1884: MS. Berg Collection, New
    York Public Library.
23. To Norton, 13 April 1884: MS. Harvard.
24. To Julia Stephen, 21 April 1885: MS. Berg.
25. To same, 22 January 1883: MS. ibid.
26. For a good general assessment, see Annan, pp. 278–86.
27. Below, p. 8.
28. To Norton, 12 May 1885; see also to same, 20 June 1881: MSS.
    Harvard.
29. To Norton, 5 March 1876: MS. Harvard, supplementing Mait-
    land, pp. 286–8.
30. To Julia Duckworth, 20 July 1877: MS. Berg. See also below, p.
    14.
31. To same, 22 July 1877: MS. Berg.
32. 2 August 1877: *The George Eliot Letters*, ed. Gordon S. Haight, VI
    (1955), p. 398.
33. To her sister, 26 May 1877: *With Dearest Love to All*, ed. Mary Reed
    Bobbitt (1960), p. 134
34. To Julia Duckworth, 3 and 5 April 1877: MSS. Berg.
35. To Norton, 30 July 1877: MS. Harvard, supplementing Maitland,
    pp. 301–2.
36. To Julia Duckworth, 14 August 1877: MS. Berg. See also below,
    p. 44.
37. Hester Thackeray Fuller and Violet Hammersley, *Thackeray's
    Daughter* (1951), p. 156. On Anny, see also Virginia Woolf's
    affectionate essay of 1924, 'The Enchanted Organ' in her
    Collected Essays, IV (1967), pp. 73–5.
38. To Norton, 25 August 1895: MS. Harvard. Similar feelings
    were expressed on 21 December—'I cannot say that I do hope
    for [her marriage], for it would be a shock to me': MS. ibid. Hills
    is first mentioned in a letter to Julia of 8 November 1891: MS. Berg.
39. To Norton, 23 August 1896: MS. Harvard; below, p. 101.
40. To Stella Hills, 10 April 1897: MS. Berg.
41. To Norton, 25 July 1897: MS. Harvard.
42. Quentin Bell, *Bloomsbury* (1968), p. 27. See also Virginia Woolf,
    Moments of Being, pp. 124–5, and Quentin Bell, *Virginia Woolf*, I,
    62–3.
43. To Norton, 3 April 1898: MS. Harvard.

44. *With Dearest Love to All*, p. 240.
45. To Julia Stephen, [30 July 1893]: MS. Berg.
46. To same, 30 January 1894: MS. ibid.
47. Vanessa Bell, *Notes on Virginia's Childhood*, ed. R. J. Schaubeck (1974), pp. [9–10].
48. To Norton, 31 December 1900: MS. Harvard.
49. *Moments of Being*, p. 110.
50. Ibid., p. 161.
51. *Scrutiny* (1941), p. 297.
52. Compare also Stephen's musings on the duration of literary eminence—pages 95–6 below—with Mr. Ramsay's reflections in part I, chapter 6 of *To the Lighthouse*.
53. Virginia Woolf, *A Writer's Diary* (1953), under 28 November 1928; see also *Moments of Being*, p. 81.
54. Virginia Woolf, 'Leslie Stephen' (1932) in *Collected Essays*, IV. 76–80; below, p. 74; George Meredith, *Collected Letters*, ed. C. L. Cline (1968), 23 February 1904. See also M. Y. Shaheen, 'A Meredith Letter to Leslie Stephen' (of 6 May 1895), *Notes and Queries* (Jan. 1977), p. 38.

THE MAUSOLEUM BOOK

4 July 1895

I AM about to copy here a paper which I wrote last May. You will find the original in a manuscript book, which I have placed in the box containing my correspondence with Julia. I shall probably make a few alterations, some of them in consequence of remarks that have occurred to me upon again looking through our letters. But unless any special reason occurs, I shall not think it worth while to mark any changes.

L.S.

---

22 Hyde Park Gate, 21 May 1895

I AM about to try to write something for my darling Julia's children: George Herbert, Stella, and Gerald de l'Etang Duckworth; and Vanessa, Julian Thoby, Adeline Virginia and Adrian Leslie Stephen. I can as yet think of nothing but the beloved wife who died on 5 May, scarcely more than a fortnight ago. I have been going over old letters and putting them in order. They have revived many old thoughts and memories of the past. Although I am, as far as I know, in good health physically, I do not feel equal to taking up my old tasks again. Yet as I am strong enough for some little employment, I think that I cannot do better than to try to fix for myself and you some of the thoughts that have occurred to me. I am so much of a professional author that I fear that what I am about to say may have the appearance of being meant rather for a book than for a letter. That, however, will be accidental if it happens—at any rate it will be unintentional. I am writing to you personally, my beloved children—for you are all beloved children to me—and I want simply to talk to you about your mother. What I shall say, therefore, is absolutely confidential between you and me. I mean to speak freely of things which are not only confidential now but which must always continue to be confidential. I have a sort of superstitious dislike (or is it the reverse of superstitious?) to giving any orders about what is to happen after I am dead. I think that the living should settle all things without having their hands tied. Consequently I will not say positively that I forbid you to make any use of this when I am dead. Indeed it might possibly be worth while for somebody to look through what I have written and make some use of it, if anything at all has to be said about me.* I intend however that this document shall remain absolutely private among us eight as long as I live. I mean further to write in such a way as to put out of the question any larger use of it than I have indicated, even after my death. Having said so much, I leave the whole matter to you.

I wish to write mainly about your mother. But I find that in order to speak intelligibly it will be best to begin by saying something about myself. It may interest you and it will make the main story clearer. Now I have no intention of writing autobiography except in this incidental way. One reason is that my memory for facts is far from a good one, and that I really remember very few incidents which are at all worth telling. Another reason is that I could give you none of those narratives of inward events, conversions or spiritual crises which give interest to some autobiographers. I was amused lately by reading Horatio Brown's life of Symonds, virtually an auto-biography, and reflecting how little of the same kind of internal history could be told of me. My mental and moral development followed a quiet and commonplace course enough. I do, indeed, remember certain facts about myself. I could give a history of some struggles through which I had to pass—successfully or otherwise: but I have a certain sense of satisfaction in reflecting that I shall take that knowledge with me to the grave. There was nothing unusual or remarkable about my inner life; although I may also say that without a knowledge of the facts to which I have referred, nobody could write an adequate history of my life. As the knowledge is confined to me and will never be imparted by me to others, it follows that no adequate history of my life can ever be written. The world will lose little by that.

* The only living person who could say anything to the purpose at present would be F. W. Maitland. He as I always feel understands me, and I have explained my views upon this subject to him. But even he could only write a short article or 'appreciation' or a notice in a biographical dictionary. No 'life' in the ordinary sense is possible.

As to the external circumstances of my early life you will find a sufficient indication of their general character in the life of my brother, Sir J. F. Stephen. It gives the best picture that I could draw of the household in which I spent my days till I went to College. I will only add that living as I did at home, where my sister and I were close companions, we two formed an especially warm intimacy which has lasted till now. I have given some account of the following period in my life of Henry Fawcett, my closest friend during the greater part of the 14 years which I spent at Cambridge. I shall just say what will enable you, if you desire it, to fill up a gap or two.

I had been kept at home on account of delicate health until I went to Cambridge (October 1850). (I ought perhaps to except a few months passed with my Aunt and Uncle Dicey in London, while I was at King's College with my two elder cousins.) My education after leaving Eton at the end of 1846 was much interrupted, owing to my own feebleness and my father's breakdown. At Cambridge I managed to do well enough to get a tutorship and fellowship at my College— Trinity Hall. The standard there was low and I was twentieth Wrangler in 1854. In order to qualify for my position it was necessary that I should take orders. I took this step rather— perhaps I should say very—thoughtlessly. I was in a vague kind of way a believer in Maurice or in what were called 'Broad Church' doctrines. My real motive was that I was very anxious to relieve my father of the burthen of supporting me.*
By taking the tutorship I became independent and after taking my degree I never cost my father anything. I was, for a time, very much attached to Cambridge. I had many friends, as you may partly see from my life of Fawcett; I was popular with my pupils, being young—at first, indeed, as young as many of them—and very anxious to avoid the fault of 'donnishness'. Some of them, like my friend Romer, now judge, have spoken gratefully of what they call my influence. I had however no influence of the kind possessed by such men as Jowett. My chief means of keeping up familiarity with the undergraduates was my interest in the boat-club and in various athletic pursuits. Though I have never been anything but

* You will see in my life of Fitzjames a reference to my father's anxieties at this time, which may help to explain my feelings.

physically weak, I had become, let us say, 'wiry'. I could walk
and run long distances and I coached our boat till it became
head of the river. In those early days, too, I became a member
of the Alpine Club, then just started, and caught an enthusiasm
which lasted many years. I was all the prouder of my athletic
performances, such as they were, because I had been regarded
as a weakling until I had taken my degree.

These are trifles, though they may help you to understand
some things about me. It is more to the purpose that I was a
liberal after the fashion of those days: a follower of J. S. Mill, like
my friend Fawcett, and, unlike Fawcett, a reader of Mill's
Logic as well as of his *Political Economy*. I read a little philosophy
—Kant, Hamilton, etc.—and was supposed at Cambridge,
where the standard was very low, to know something about it.
I read Comte, too, and became convinced among other things
that Noah's flood was a fiction (or rather convinced that I had
never believed in it) and that it was wrong for me to read the
story as if it were a sacred truth. So I had to give up my position
at Trinity Hall. Upon my stating in the summer of 1862 that I
could no longer take part in the chapel services, I resigned my
tutorship at the request of the Master. The college, however,
allowed me to retain my fellowship and hold some minor
offices.* I remained at Cambridge two years longer as bursar,
steward, etc., made a trip to the United States in 1863, where I
had the great good fortune of forming a friendship with Lowell,
and finally left the place at the end of 1864. My last two years of
residence were a mistake—I became heartily sick of University
life, which had now become objectless enough, and resolved to
take up literature as a profession.

Here I must make one remark about myself. It will perhaps
strike you, who have only known me at a much later period, as
inapplicable. But though it describes a state of mind which I
have long left behind it was long true. Indeed, I am not sure
that in some respects it has passed away so completely as I
suggest. This remark is that I was less given than most people
to any forethought as to my future. I never speculated as to

---

* This, I believe, was due in great part to Fawcett. I refer to the fact in my life of him,
where I speak also of being able to return his good offices at Christmas 1866. I may add
that from a letter of mine to H. M. Thackeray of 26 December 1866, I find that in the
book I must have rather underestimated the opposition which I then had to encounter.

what was to happen to me, but took things as they came. I well remember my dear mother asking me—about the time, I suppose, of my abandoning my old career—'What are your plans?' I replied that I had none. I did not care to see my way for more than a few months in advance.

How it came to pass that I, who am of rather anxious temperament, and who have always had a strong sense of the importance of making use of my time (for that I have had), should have been so indifferent is a problem which I leave to you. I could say something which might help to clear it up. But I could only do so by making some of those personal disclosures from which I have resolved to refrain. In fact it matters little.

Anyhow I came to London at the end of 1864 intending to support myself by my pen. I had already made an experiment or two with fair success. I calculated that I should be able, as was in fact the case, to make easily enough to supply my wants as a bachelor. At Cambridge I had learnt to consider myself as rather an old bachelor. I looked no further. For the next two years, 1865-6, I lived quietly with my mother and sister at 19 Porchester Square. We had, as you may guess, a very quiet household, and my life was peaceful and happy.

Here I must observe that I started as a journalist with many advantages. My brother was, as he had been for several years, a leading Saturday Reviewer. At the beginning of 1865 he was also taking a prominent part in the *Pall Mall Gazette*, then just started. (For the story of these papers see my life of Fitzjames.) Through him I was of course easily introduced to the editors of both papers and I became a regular writer in them for some years. It was not a very exalted profession; but at that time I felt, naturally, more respect for a literary life—perhaps I should only say for the career of a journalist—than I can feel now. I was proud of taking even a secondary place in the leading papers of the day; and was somehow not discontented at the thought that I was devoting my whole energy to merely ephemeral production, though, indeed, I am not quite sure that I had not even then vague thoughts of writing something more ambitious. However I was perfectly content with my position, which had the advantage of bringing me into occasional contact with some of the leading writers of the time. My want of memory for facts would make it impossible for me, even if I wished to do so, to give you 'reminiscences' of the ordinary kind. I knew various people of more or less reputation, some of whom are mentioned in the life of Fitzjames. I saw something of Fawcett's friends, Cairnes and W. T. Thornton, the economists, and even of the great J. S. Mill: I came to know Tennyson and Browning and Mat. Arnold; I knew Carlyle (though I was always afraid of him without any cause except his fame) and Froude, the last two through my brother; I knew G. H. Lewes and Mrs. Lewes (George Eliot) and old Anthony Trollope and Huxley and Herbert Spencer—and I pass by all these names, telling you nothing of them and, indeed, having little to tell. All that I have named died before this was written, except the last two. (And today (4 July) I have been to Huxley's funeral also.) Huxley was always a good friend: he has more than once of late held out a very kind hand to me, and though very ill at the time of my darling's death, sent me an affectionate message by his wife's hand. I have rarely seen him since his retirement to Eastbourne: but I have a cordial affection for him—alas! I must now say, for his memory.

I simply mention these names to show you that in these years (1865 and succeeding years) I had the opportunity of knowing most of the literary people of mark. I joined the Cosmopolitan, then and I believe still a famous resort for the select intellects of London, and a smaller society on the same plan called the Century. To it belonged many of the clever young writers and barristers, chiefly of the radical persuasion. I chiefly remember Fred. Harrison and some of his positivist friends. We used to meet on Wednesday and Sunday evenings, to smoke and drink in moderation and discuss the Universe and the Reform movement of 1866–7. A volume of Essays on reform, published about this time, contains an essay of mine, which, I remember, appeared to me to be very good. I have not looked at it for years; but the volume would give you, if you cared to look at it, some notion of our general tone. I wonder whether the Century has entirely vanished? I left both it and the Cosmopolitan many years ago—after 1875 when, as I shall have to tell you, I became too much of a recluse to enjoy such gatherings.

And now I reach an important passage in my domestic history. I must speak of it with some fulness, in order that you may understand my life. I do not, however, mean to dwell upon it so much as upon the later story with which you are more closely connected. W. M. Thackeray had died at Christmas 1863, leaving two daughters, Anny and Minny (whose real names were Anne Isabella, b. 1837, and Harriet Marian, b. 1840) to live with his mother. A year later, his mother followed him. The daughters went to live by themselves at a little house at 16 Onslow Gardens. They were known to my mother and sister. Fitzjames had been on friendly terms with Thackeray, and Thackeray had accepted several articles of his for the *Cornhill Magazine*. George Smith, Thackeray's publisher, had been very kind to the daughters; they were often at his house (he was then living at Hampstead) and Smith, as proprietor of the *Pall Mall Gazette*, knew me and often asked me to dinners where he entertained various literary people. The Thackerays again were especially intimate with Herman Merivale, who had succeeded my father at the Colonial Office and was a man of high reputation both in an official and a literary capacity. (His life is in the *Dicty. of Nat. Biog.*) I cannot remember whether I was introduced to him by the Thackerays or knew him already. Anyhow, having so many common friends I soon came to know the Thackerays. I vividly remember how they came to luncheon with my mother at Porchester Square and how I talked about novels to Anny and how I ingeniously observed that I liked my old favourites best; and, upon being asked what novel then was my favourite, replied *Vanity Fair*. I was speaking the truth and hope that she saw it.

And so I had and took the chance of falling in love with my darling Minny. Once in the early days I dined with the Smiths at Hampstead, when she sat next to me. Another guest was Mrs. Gaskell the novelist. I remember still, though I shall not repeat them, some words of my conversation with Minny. Mrs. Gaskell, as I was told, said afterwards that she then foresaw that Minny Thackeray would become my wife. It is probable enough that our mutual feelings were sufficiently transparent to a looker-on. And yet in the rather odd state of mind of which I have spoken, the growth of my feeling was slower than might have been anticipated. I was shy, diffident, and fully impressed with the conviction acquired at Cambridge that I was an old don—a superannuated bachelor standing apart from all thought of domestic happiness. Nor, in fact, so far as I can remember had we very frequent opportunities of meeting in the early days. It was only upon looking back from some interval of time that I wondered that the distance between us had not lessened more rapidly. I will describe to you two or three little memory pictures which may sufficiently indicate our story. One is of a picnic somewhere in the Leith Hill country in 1866. Anny and Minny had taken lodgings at a farm-house there and had asked a party to come down, stroll about and have some sort of entertainment at (I am pretty sure) Abinger Hatch. Of this I shall have to speak again presently. I only mention now how I then began to perceive that Minny was somehow drawing nearer to me. I must have perceived it, indeed, before this; but this particular occasion was a kind of revelation to me: it marked a distinct step in advance. She showed a gentle pleasure when the accidents of the day brought us together. I was soon looking forwards to another meeting which was happily accomplished. A great friend of the Thackerays was kind Mrs. Huth. Her husband Henry Huth (1815–78, see *Dicty. of Nat. Biog.*) was a rich German merchant and a great collector of books: his library is famous among bibliophiles. Mrs. Huth was 'intellectual' and worshipped Buckle, who took her sons with him upon his last journey. After Buckle's death, Mrs. Huth tried worshipping Herbert Spencer: but whether she did not offer or he did not care for the right kind of worship, they never, I think, became equally intimate. Mrs. Huth had some of the weaknesses of the worshippers of intellect, but she was a good kind woman. She liked to collect clever people at her house and had been naturally drawn to the Thackerays. She took moreover a special fancy to Minny and tried—not very successfully—to make her read Buckle. She used to talk 'philosophy' and put what my Minny calls 'corkscrewing' questions to her young friend; and—to do her justice—was not in the least repelled by the failure to elicit much response. Mrs. Huth was going for a trip to Switzerland this year: she invited Anny and Minny to join her, and I promised to meet them. I fancy that Mrs. Huth and other persons concerned had some inkling of what was likely to result from a meeting. I went to Zermatt—the trysting-place—alone. The Huths went first to Chamonix; and my Minny used afterwards to tell how she had dragged the whole party thence to Zermatt and how Anny had said to her, 'You must really not ask every young Alpine traveller, where is Mr. Leslie Stephen?' I meanwhile heard one day of their approach and walked down the valley to meet them. One of my sacred places ever afterwards was a point where the road winds round a little bluff near Täsch. Thence I descried the party approaching on mules—there was then no railway or even carriage-road—and I walked back with them to Zermatt. I passed there two or three days of the happiest and took my Minny (not then mine) upon the Görner Glacier and up to the Riffel. How well I remember sitting on a little grassy platform under the Riffel-Horn with Anny, Minny and Miss Huth! I began to know that my fate was fixed. Yet, rather perversely, I chose to keep an engagement which I had made with Bryce (already known by his *Roman Empire*) and went with him to Vienna (where I first met George Meredith) and Transylvania. I returned in the autumn to London and still for a time waited and hesitated; not that I was not in love, but that I was still troubled by some of my old doubts and diffidence. Indeed I heard at last some sort of rumour that Minny or Anny felt some annoyance at my conduct. One day, therefore, I lunched by myself at the Oxford and Cambridge Club; thought over the whole affair in a philosophical spirit; and went to 16 Onslow Gardens, where I found Minny alone and made her a little speech which I had carefully thought out, setting forth all my feelings and the reasons for the offer with which I concluded. Her simple 'Yes' dispersed all memory of the 'reasons'. There was one quite sufficient reason! We were engaged towards the end of 1866 (4 December, I find). Our marriage did not take place till 19 June 1867. The interval during our engagement was one of exquisite happiness: and so, with hardly an exception, was the period, eight years and a half, of our married life.

I must speak to you a little of that life, my dear children, though with a strange feeling. It all seems to me so far away and yet so vivid. To you it can be but as the vague indication of a dream. That was the time when our happiness could still be youthful, buoyant, marred by no misgiving or painful foreboding. How can I describe my Minny to you? You may see her portrait by Watts in my study. It is a sweet picture. I got him to make a copy of it after my darling's death; the copy was my wedding-present to Anny upon her marriage in 1877 to Richmond Ritchie. It fails in my opinion to preserve the likeness satisfactorily. You can, in my picture at any rate, trace Minny's likeness both to her father and to her sister. The most striking features, I think, were the beautiful eyes—the form inherited, I think, from her father and beautiful in form rather than in colour. They were a blue-gray. I do not think that she could be called beautiful; but the face was interesting and attractive to me (I fancy not to me alone! but I speak for myself) from the first. Dear Anny could never be called good-looking—unless the word mean looking good—and Minny was very like her, but very superior in appearance if judged by the ordinary rules. Anny's face was always ill-drawn or clumsy, though singularly amiable and intelligent: Minny was like her *minus* the clumsiness. Now you know Anny and I think that I can best tell you what I care to tell about Minny by first speaking of Anny. Her influence upon my life, too, was great enough to require some notice of her. Anny inherited no small share of her father's genius, but with differences which I attribute, or think attributable, to her Irish blood. She is still, she was, I think, still more obviously when I first knew her, the most sympathetic person I ever knew. By 'sympathetic' I mean able to sympathize quickly with the feelings of all manner of people, to throw herself into their interests and thoughts and even for a time adopt their opinions. I have never observed such readiness, such accessibility to appeals from others, in any human being. Since her marriage her feelings have had to flow in a narrower channel and this quality is perhaps rather less conspicuous. Its manifestation led people of more impassive temperament to occasional doubts of her sincerity—doubts which were utterly unjust so far as they implied any question of her conscious sincerity. She could not always live up to the strength of her momentary impulses, or feel always all that she felt at times— no one heart could have room for so many emotions: but she said no more than she actually felt at any given time. Some of the prejudices, fancies and so forth which she had accepted, as it were, by reflection from other minds faded when the object was no longer in front of the mirror. But the affection remained.

No kinder-hearted person ever lived. Fitzjames and I in those days called her a 'sentimentalist', a name which in our mouths implied some blame. Yet she was not only free from any insincerity, except such as might result from a too facile yielding to her impulses, but she had another quality which saved her from being sentimental in any really bad sense. This was the quality inherited from her father and which led to the popular complaints of his 'cynicism'. I spare you any attempt at analysing the meaning of the word. He had had a very trying life which, as I guess, gave a bitter edge to some of his feelings. She resembled him in so far as this, that she had a decided sense of humour, a distinct perception of the weak side of people even whom she loved, and—though absolutely without bitterness—could see the seamy side of things too clearly to be quite carried away by sentimentalism. She dealt rather too freely in rose-colour; but her sweetness was just flavoured with acidity. There was in her books an underlying strain of what, though not cynical, had a certain affinity to the (so-called) cynicism of her father. This made a very interesting and characteristic way of looking at things: extreme kindliness, crossed and blended with a vein of subsatirical humour. It redeemed her from the charge of sentimentalism in the eyes of rather harder and dryer people, like myself. She had, however, and has, a characteristic which always made a difference between us and which I cannot unreservedly applaud. She has, that is, an extraordinary capacity for looking (as it is called) at the bright side of things. It is too like a reluctance to look painful facts in the face— a weakness, though an amiable weakness! I always have to discount her statements, when we speak of expectations of coming events. 'I am so glad', she will say, telling me of something that she has observed, or supposes herself to have observed, in the state of those whom she loves, and when she gives me the reasons for gladness, I often see in them reason for anxiety or sorrow. She really, I take it, hates sorrow and tries to put it aside. In moments of depression, this excessive optimism jars upon me to whom a melancholy view comes more naturally.

I must say a word of her intellectually. Her mind was even oddly unmethodical. She was never educated systematically and she always gives one the impression of being in a muddle about facts and figures. ('There are forty millions of unmarried women in London alone!' she once declared to me.) This is a real defect and it has, I think, been very injurious to her books. She showed more perception and humour, more delicate and tender and beautiful emotion, than would have made the fortune of a dozen novelists, had she had her faculties more in hand. Had she, for example, as I often thought, had any share of Miss Austen's gift for clearness, proportion and neatness, her books would have been much better and incomparably more successful. As it is, partly from a want of proper focussing, partly from her desire to put things picturesquely and consequent reluctance to give the proper detail of commonplace fact, her books were often hard to follow. Once when a story of hers was published in Australia, the last chapter got into the middle and nobody found it out—in Australia, at any rate. She wrote fragments as thoughts struck her and pinned them (with literal not metaphorical pins) at odd parts of her MS., till it became a chaotic jumble, maddening to the printers. I remember how old Trollope (who was free from *that* fault!) and G. Smith and I used to entreat for a little more orderly arrangement of her plots, the relationship of her characters and so forth; but I saw in time that such criticism only bothered her and did no good. I found the other day an odd letter from my brother (written about 1864 or 5) exhorting her to read systematically through Macaulay and Gibbon and Hallam and such people. It was well-meant advice, but, as I could have afterwards told him, utterly useless.

Well, this literary defect was partly represented in her life; but, as I have said of her sentimentalism, with a curious compensation. Unsystematic and confused as her statements might be about business and so forth, she yet had always a strong substratum of common sense. She often enough gave absurd or contradictory reasons but she generally came to sound conclusions. This was partly due to the extreme frankness with which she would ask advice and throw herself upon others for help; partly to the quickness with which she recognized the good qualities of her advisers: but also to the fact that she had really sound abilities, which somehow enabled her to work round to sound opinions by intricate and apparently absurd processes.

Everybody who knew her loved her. Her extreme openness, her quick sympathies and her bright perceptions made her one of the most delightful of persons in all social intercourse. On all occasions of that kind she was invaluable; her only fault being that her mind was a little too active in jumping from one topic to another and so sometimes throwing the talk out of gear. But she was exceedingly popular and everyone who could appreciate kindness and sympathy and simplicity combined with real brilliancy sought for her company.

I have digressed a little: partly, perhaps, because, as I find from my letters, when Anny lived with me, I was constantly framing theories to account for her. You see the result. But it is also true, as I said, that anything I can say of Minny must start by a reference to Anny. The sisters, when I first knew them, were living quietly together, reviving from the sadness caused by the deaths of their father and grandmother, and taking their part in a social life of which I shall speak presently. The relation between them might be compared to the relation between a popular author and his wife. My Minny, of course, played the part of wife in the little household. That is, she was to all appearance entirely dependent upon her sister. She both loved Anny and believed in her with the most unstinted warmth. I shall never forget how my excellent brother tried after his fashion (he was not very scrupulous about helping a friend in the press—or elsewhere) to do Anny a kindness by reviewing one of her stories in *Fraser* ('The Village on the Cliff' I fancy). This was in 1867 when Minny had just become my wife. Fitzjames's article was very well meant, but he had not the light touch necessary for criticism of such delicate wares; and all that he could manage to write was a proper comparison of Anny to Miss Austen, with ponderous insistence upon the negative merits of absence of improprieties, sensationalism and so forth. I gave the article to Minny in the train as we were going to Anny's cottage at Henley after our wedding-trip. I remember her indignation. 'Fitzy', she exclaimed, 'does not see that Anny is a genius!' It was true; and Minny did appreciate Anny to the very core of her heart. This may lead to what I want to say, though I find it very hard to say it properly. My Minny had far less intellectual power than Anny: she tried, I know, to write little stories, but she did not get very far with them.* Yet she had, I fancy, inherited more of her father's intellectual temperament, though less of his intellectual force. She was without what I have called Anny's Irish qualities. She was more reserved and less impulsive by nature and without Anny's peculiar gift of sympathy. Her sense of humour was more predominant, if not precisely stronger, and enabled her to see some things more clearly. She had not the peculiar, or, as I thought, excessive optimism which I have ascribed to Anny. She judged by her instincts, for she was not more of a reasoner than Anny; but her instincts were calmer and more sober. The quality which first of all attracted me was one which she also shared with Anny, but which was more obvious in her from her less impulsive temperament: I mean an absolute and unqualified simplicity and sincerity in which I never saw her surpassed. She was utterly incapable not only (like Anny) of ever affecting, but (unlike Anny) of ever appearing to affect, a sentiment which she did not feel. Her simplicity was the simplicity of a child and she remained, in some ways, a child through life. She was no more capable than a perfectly unspoilt child of assuming even for an instant any impulse which was not thoroughly genuine. And then her nature was one of quiet love: of a sort of complacent indulgence of tender, cherishing, caressing emotions towards those dearest to her. I had never seen any one, I used to think, not even a woman, whose manner to children was so perfect. She made no ostentation of special appreciation of children, but showed herself to children just as she was—tender, gentle, affectionate, capable of entering naturally into all their little amusements and pleasures. Almost her only attempt to go beyond her domestic circle was due to her interest in stories which she had seen in the papers of the ill-treatment of children. She tried to help some who had been neglected or harshly treated by their parents and one—a

* 10 April 1897. An odd little incident has just happened. Smith & Elder bought at a sale an old *Cornhill* proofsheet with a fable. It had been carefully corrected by Thackeray and was described by the sellers as a 'suppressed' story by him. It had never been published, and they found no trace of it in their books. Upon reading it, I saw at once that it was not by W.M.T.: the style was obviously immature. It was also obvious that he had for some reason taken a special interest in it. I have very little doubt that it was written by Minny. He probably had thought that he could make it do, but changed his mind. Anny remembers nothing about it, but thinks my guess probable. The wise S. & E. imagined that it had some political meaning, but it was really a simple little fable about a fox and a monk and so forth.

certain 'Sammy' Somers—has been a kind of client of mine till now. Julia looked after him in later years and he is in a decent position. I remember how once at the Zoological Gardens I looked at one of the beautiful little foxes and said 'you are like my Minny', and how Fitzjames agreed with me. Its 'cunning' (in the American sense) and apparently amiable little face reminded me of her expression. To make a better comparison you may see in the drawing-room an engraving after Sir Joshua's 'Lady Caroline Montagu'—Thackeray bought another copy (which went to Anny) because it reminded him of his little daughter. When I married Julia, Lowell sent me a cheque to buy a wedding-present which I spent upon the copy now belonging to me, and whenever I look at it, I see the likeness. I bought the engraving of the 'Countess Spencer'— also after Sir Joshua—because it suggested to me the same rather vague likeness of my Minny's bright expression. Perhaps you may derive from them some impression of my impression. When I call her childlike, I think of the thorough fearlessness, simplicity and straightforwardness of a child, who is tender and loving by nature, who has lived with tender and loving people and developed with absolute naturalness. She might have convinced her father (I dare say she did!) that there are natures in which even the germs of his pet vice of 'snobbishness' do not exist. A lady said to me after her death, 'she was the most pure minded woman I ever knew'. She was pure minded as happily many women are pure minded, in the ordinary sense of the word—free from the very slightest taint of any coarseness of feeling: but I apply the word to her in a wider sense. Her emotions were absolutely free from the alloy of self-consciousness, conceit or desire for meaner things which destroys the true ring of the natural affections. Although she was not widely educated and had no remarkable intellectual force, she impressed me from the very beginning with the conviction that there was no sentiment in her mind which she cared to conceal or which it could be desirable for her to conceal in the very slightest degree. To picture her to myself is now, more than ever, like looking into the very soul of a sweet child, brought up in the pure atmosphere of a quiet home and responding to every influence of domestic affection. To know her and her sister was to strengthen my regard for the father, whom I had never personally known, to whom they owed so much and whom they loved so dearly. To live with such a woman and to feel that her affection for me was strengthening and deepening was an inestimable happiness. I will just add what my friend Lowell wrote about her to some one who copied his words for Anny and me: 'Mrs. Stephen's death', he said, 'goes to my heart. She was one of the most natural human beings I ever knew, and her humour was as quaint as it was constant in its flow, yet always incalculable beforehand.

'Something of Thackeray was in that, but this
Was all of him with whom she is now in bliss.'

(The quotation, I think, a little obscure!) 'And Stephen was so in love with her, and delighted in her so. It was a renewal of youth to see them together.' To me he said in a touching letter of the same time: 'I cannot bear to think of it. Seldom can a stroke wound so many and so deeply. But you *loved* her, thank God!' Yes, I loved her.*

* From *Autobiography of a Journalist* (W. J. Stillman) 1901. Vol 2, p. 93: 'I brought with me from Lowell a letter to Leslie Stephen, whose friendship has ever since been one of the pleasantest things in my English life. Mrs. Stephen, the elder (younger–L.S.) daughter of Thackeray, was to us an angel of goodness and never since has the grateful recognition of her loving hospitality in thought and deed diminished in my mind. Our debt to her was a debt of the heart and those are never paid. Her sister, later Mrs. Ritchie, added much to the obligations of our early life in London and still remains our friend.'

(This refers to Minny's helping Stillman to see Marie Spartali, to whom he was then engaged. Her father objected to the marriage and we used to bring about meetings in our house at 16 Onslow Gardens—about 1870. Stillman is a good fellow and this reminiscence touches me.) I wrote to him to say that I had been pleased, had a note from his wife with a message in answer from him, and two days later heard of his death. (6 July 1901.)

Here is a bit from Mrs. Simpson's *Many Memories of Many People* (1898), p. 109: 'No one who knew intimately Thackeray's younger daughter, Mrs. L.S., could ever forget her. The heroine in her sister's novel *Old Kensington* must have been drawn from her. Her beautiful bronze hair, brilliantly white teeth and delicate complexion one minute with the soft tint of the china rose and then again white as a lily, gave one the impression of the most exquisite freshness. One day she would look like the young girl she really was and, on the next, twenty years older, so varying were her moods and expression. To those with whom she felt no sympathy, she appeared cold and reserved, for she was sincere almost to bluntness: but beneath this exterior was a most tender and loving heart. She was one of those people who do not *like*; they love and are beloved in return. She probably possessed the literary talent of her family, for her letters were most entertaining and her conversation full of fun. She and I became much attracted to each other. We did all sorts of things together: we got up a Latin class, and shared a district, besides the frivolous amusements that I have already described.' (i.e. 'cooking party' and acting—H. she says was a 'first-rate actress'.)

I don't very well follow some of this: but it is kindly meant and pleased A. T. Ritchie.

Here I must say one thing more. You know the tragedy of
Thackeray's life. After my Minny's birth (28 May 1840) her
mother had a fever; the fever affected her brain and after a
period of anxiety she had finally to be put under care. She never
recovered and lived in a state of dreamlike incapacity until 1893
—always, I may add, carefully looked after by Anny. Now I
knew something of this and a vague dread had occurred to me
that Minny might not be without some hereditary taint. The
facts, however, seemed to put this out of the question, as it
seemed to be clear that the mischief was due to the accidental
illness after Minny's birth. Yet I have sometimes fancied that
there was something not altogether erroneous in the general
impression. 'Aunt Jane', as we used to call her, Mrs. Thackeray's
elder sister, was so queer as to be almost on the borders of
sanity: and thoughts of this kind were suggested, as I need
hardly tell you, by the later history of my poor little Laura.
There was not, however, the very slightest suspicion of this
kind during Minny's life in my own mind, nor, I fancy, in the
mind of any one else. Neither can I recall anything which
could be regarded as a symptom of such a calamity. On the
contrary, I thought, and I still think, that, within her own sphere
of thoughts and interests, Minny always showed herself
singularly sane and sensible in her practical judgements and
took a wise estimate of life and of the people with whom she
had to do. Her charm, however, depended upon that rare and
exquisite quality of character which I have clumsily tried to
describe. She was a poem, though not a poetess; she had a
harmonious and beautifully balanced disposition; and that
childlikeness (the reverse of childishness) of which I have
spoken always dwells in my memory and gives an unspeakable
charm to my vision of the eight years and a half (1867–75)
during which she was my beloved wife.

I shall now go briefly over the little events of this period, not as
important or interesting in themselves, but as they may help
you to picture our little story more distinctly.

We lived for some years after our marriage in the little house
(16 Onslow Gardens) where Anny and Minny were already
settled; and Anny continued to live with us. My occupations
went on as before. I wrote regularly for the *Pall Mall Gazette*
and for the *Saturday Review*. I remember Minny's pleasure when

the editor of the *Saturday* gave me a sort of retaining fee of fifty guineas a year by way, as he said, of wedding-present. I did a little for Froude, then editor of *Fraser's Magazine* and in the beginning of 1871, the Longmans offered to take me as his successor. I consulted G. Smith who thereupon offered me the *Cornhill* which I accepted the more willingly from its connection with Thackeray. I began my duties with the March number of 1871, and though the pay (£500 a year) was not magnificent, it enabled me to give up some of my journalism and to set about a book—the so-called *History of English Thought in the Eighteenth Century*. I wrote it with a certain audacity which I do not now possess. I took some things very easily, as it seems to me, and subsequent work requiring more thorough research has led me to guess that the book was in many ways very superficial. But that is a trifle.

I will now give a few hints as to the domestic life which went on so happily in these years. My Minny shared my love of the Alps. She was not, indeed, a walker but she heartily enjoyed the life and the scenery. We spent our honeymoon in Switzerland, revisiting, among other places, the scene of our meeting at Zermatt in the previous year. Anny had thought it desirable to have some independent establishment, although she meant to be also a regular inmate of our house. She accordingly took a cottage at Henley, whither, as I have said, we went for a short visit after our return to England. But the scheme proved too expensive and the life at Henley too secluded. Anny accordingly gave up the plan and took up her abode with us, if it should not rather be said that we took up our abode with her. She was certainly the most conspicuous figure in the house. In 1868 I went with my darling Minny to America, and there renewed my friendship with Lowell and others. In 1869 we went, partly for her health, to the Alps again; and in my *Playground of Europe* you will find descriptions of the baths of Santa Catarina——where Minny was supposed to be taking the waters—and of Primiero. We spent some delicious weeks at the two places. In 1870 came the war between France and Prussia. Minny was expecting her confinement and suffered a good deal of discomfort. We took a little house on the Thames near Kingston and went afterwards to Bramley, near Guildford, where my mother and sister were spending the summer. There I made the

acquaintance of Morley, then living on the Hog's Back. I made
a rush to the Alps, passing through France and returning by the
Rhine in the midst of the war. Laura Makepeace was born
(prematurely) on 7 December 1870. She was a very delicate
child, but was carried through her infantile troubles by her
mother's intense tenderness and unremitting care. We had a
happy life afterwards. We spent the summer of 1871 at St.
Gervais, ending with a short stay at Chamonix. In 1872 we
decided, I forget why, to stay at home. We took a farmhouse,
called Rosemerrin, belonging to the Miss Sterlings and close
to their house, The Crag, near Falmouth. My sister came to stay
with us there and fell in love with the Quakers—a very important event in her history. I made another of my rushes to the
Alps, returning to Cornwall. In 1873 we all—Anny, Minny,
Laura and I—had a delightful time at old Cousset's Inn at
Chamonix. I climbed Mont Blanc to see the sunset and think—
forgive an author's vanity!—that my description in the *Cornhill*,
reprinted in the last edition of the *Playground*—is the best thing
I ever wrote and a good bit of Alpine literature. In 1874 my
mother's health was so weak that we did not like to go abroad.
We took a house at Englefield Green, near Cooper's Hill
College, at which my friend Wolstenholme was then professor.
I went, however, to the Alps once more; and with F. W. Gibbs
went to Courmayeur, where poor James Marshall had just
been killed. We had seen him at Chamonix the year before and
I had crossed the Col des Hirondelles with him. Curiously, I had
declined to try with him the expedition which afterwards led
to his death, because Minny fancied him to be an unsafe walker.
I went now to the place of the accident, and I made friends with
Victor and Julia Marshall, who had come out to see after the
grave etc. My mother died early in 1875. I have written of that
in the life of my brother, and will here say no more. Minny was
again in that summer expecting a confinement. I shall not
forget how pleased she was when her doctor told her that it
would be good for her health to spend some months in the Alps.
We went first to Interlaken and Mürren. At Mürren the cold
seemed to try her. Anny came out to us and went with her to
Grindelwald, while I returned upon *Cornhill* business to
England. I went out again and we spent our last summer
together at Grindelwald and Rosenlaui. Mrs. Oliphant with

her two sons, then promising lads, made friends with us at Grindelwald. The boys are both dead and, I fear, not much loss to the outside world. In a copy of the *Golden Treasury* which Anny gave me, I preserve an edelweiss which I gathered near Rosenlaui. It is to me now a relic, taking me back to bright days and to visions of Minny's intense delight (both on this and former visits) in playing with Laura upon sunny Alpine meadows. We returned in the autumn and, though Minny had much discomfort, no fear had crossed my mind.

One evening—27 November 1875—I was sitting at home with her in perfect happiness and security. Your mother, then Mrs. Herbert Duckworth—looked in to see us. She found us— so she afterwards told me—so happy together that she thought the presence of a desolate widow incongruous, and left us to return to her own solitary hearth. Frederick Gibbs called, too, I remember and my Minny asked him to do some little commission of kindness to—I forget who. She went to bed in some discomfort and thought it best to sleep in a room where one Mary Anne, a maid of Anny's, could keep an eye upon her. Anny was at Eton. During the night Mary Anne called me; I got up and found my darling in a convulsion. I fetched the doctor. I remember only too clearly the details of what followed; but I will not set them down. My darling never regained consciousness. She died about the middle of the day, 28 November, my forty-third birthday. You know why I have never celebrated that day! I was left alone.

My Minny was buried at Kensal Green by my father and mother, and my brother now lies by them. At Anny's suggestion we placed above the grave a slab upon which is carved a group of Alpine flowers. It was done by a poor little Italian sculptor, cheaply and, I guess, not very artistically. Yet I like the thought and I like the stone, even such as it is. I mention it because it is characteristic in one way. I always, for reasons sufficiently explained, associate my Minny with the Alps in which she and I and our child passed so many happy hours. She loved the flowers there. Some of those upon the grave are cyclamens. We had brought home some roots of the purple sweetscented cyclamen from Primiero; and I have always loved them since and taken them in their grace and sweetness as a kind of emblem of my darling. I seem always to see her as she sat with her infant in such perfect confidence under the great mountains. She had, I hope, no forebodings and no anxious thought until the blow which deprived her of consciousness. I cannot however analyse my feeling. I only know that the sweet, delicately formed, shy little cyclamen nestling in the Alpine meadow under the great cliffs somehow represents her for me. Who can say why?*

I must speak now of another matter. Anny had, as I have said, lived with us till now and continued to live with me after her sister's death. She and I had our little contentions. I had a perhaps rather pedantic mania for correcting her flights of imagination and checking her exuberant impulses. A. and M. used to call me the cold bath from my habit of drenching Anny's little schemes and fancies with chilling criticism. We were never very serious in our quarrels and had come to understand each other better—I remember her remarking upon this just after my Minny's death. She reminded me of a little set-to we had lately had. Minny in earlier days would have been alarmed. As it was, she only laughed and said, 'What are you two people making such a noise about?' I will say that in those last months I had come to feel that between me and Minny there was not only love but unbroken harmony. We seemed to recognize and to share each other's wishes and feelings at a glance. One proof is that Minny had begun to think that it might be as well for Anny to take a house of her own. If, as we expected, our family was to be increased, our scale of expenditure might require to be altered. We had a dream, I remember, of going to Brighton to follow the example and enjoy the society of John Morley, then very intimate with me. The scheme showed no decline of love for Anny, but a growing closeness to me. In the earlier days she would have dreaded the most partial separation from her sister. She now thought of it, chiefly on the ground that it might make Anny more prudent in money matters.

(I observe parenthetically that Mrs. Jackson said afterwards that my behaviour to Anny always puzzled people: but that after living in the house with us, she sympathized with me, for Anny was always the aggressor and could not keep silence.

* I shall just say that in a cabinet in the drawing-room are casts of Minny's hands. They were taken after death by desire of someone—I forget who—who thought them beautiful. I do not like such things.

Upon Julia reporting this, I confess that Anny's aggressions were not very irritating, and that she was like a person forced to live in a den with a fretful beast and persisting in stroking it the wrong way.)

Now I will make a little boast. The wisest resolution I ever made in my life was upon my marriage to Minny. Whatever happens, I said, I will not quarrel about money matters, which are, after all, the great causes of quarrel. Now in those days Anny was generous to recklessness. As soon as money came into her purse it flowed out. She occasionally received good prices for her stories; but she simply spent the more. This was no great harm so long as she was unmarried; and since her marriage her good sense has shown itself by a great improvement in economy. But in the early days of my marriage Anny received both her own income and Minny's and spent both in this lavish manner. I had then to request that Minny's share should be paid to me direct, so that it might not evaporate before I got it. This being arranged, I agreed to pay all the household expenses in the first instance and to make out an account showing Anny's debt to me. When I did this, it generally happened that she could not pay me, or had to wait till some new story had made her flush of money. I found it rather unpleasant to tell her of her debts to me. She did not quite approve of the practice. She thought or took for granted that I ought to be as careless as she was herself; and somehow it is not easy to present oneself as a creditor without appearing to be a curmudgeon. Here comes in my boast. I gave up reminding Anny of her debts, and was content to take upon myself much the largest share of the expenses—more, that is, than my proper share. I am always glad of this. From something which Anny said to me the other day, I find that she is still completely ignorant of the fact. She remembered and spoke with more than abundant gratitude of a present which I was afterwards able to make her. I gave her £500 to enable her to buy a house upon her marriage; and she talked about repaying this some day or of her children repaying mine. I mention this here, partly because I wish you to understand that should such a repayment be offered—which, I confess, strikes me as im-probable—it is not to be accepted. I am too proud, I hope, to turn any gifts of mine into loans. But I wish chiefly to say that I have no cause of regret for any of my pecuniary relations to Anny.* I avoided—I am thankful to say—that rock of offence: and though I may regret faults of temper, I cannot charge myself with a want of liberality. I shall refer to this again presently. It has some bearing upon the next period. The romance of my life was to follow; and it is of that and of the conditions of my life at the time that I have principally to dwell. Without duly appreciating them, you cannot realize what your mother was to me.

I shall begin by setting down a few facts—known already to you, my elder children, but not so fully known to the younger.

Your beloved mother, Julia Prinsep, was the third daughter of Dr. Jackson. (He was born 17 November 1804.) He was a very fine old man until his death in 1887 and had had a life of almost unbroken health. He was strongly built and had a good, sensible, kindly face, surmounted by masses of white hair. When Vanessa and Thoby were tiny, they came home one day from a call and announced with a due sense of mystery that they had found grandpapa's hair in the fireplace. It had been filled with white chips for the summer. Dr. Jackson had been educated at Catharine Hall, Cambridge and had gone to Calcutta in the twenties (I suppose). I once heard him tell of adventures by the way, whether from shipwreck or pirates—I am ashamed to say that I forget which—but he was little given to talking of himself. He prospered as a physician in Calcutta and about 1837 (I take it) married Maria Pattle. She was one of seven lovely sisters (see *Dicty. of Nat. Biog.*, art. Julia Margaret Cameron). One became wife of a General Mackenzie, one (Sara) of Henry Thoby Prinsep, one ('Aunt Loo') of H. V. Bayley, one ('Aunt Sophy') of J. W. Dalrymple, and one, Virginia—the loveliest—of Lord Somers. I have omitted the cleverest, I see, Julia Margaret, who became Mrs. Charles Hay Cameron. Their mother, Mrs. Pattle, was daughter of a

* In regard to the above statement, I have now (July 1898) a statement to make. Anny is prefacing the new edition of her father's works. Smith & Elder gave her £4000 for her share. She thereupon declared that I had a claim to part, inasmuch as the materials used by her (her father's letters, etc.) belonged equally to Minny and her. Moreover she urged that her children would inherit my share of Minny's money upon my death. She proposed therefore to pay me £800—which I began by refusing. She seemed to be so anxious to give me some that I ultimately agreed to take half this (£400). I don't know whether this was right: but—I did it.

Chevalier de l'Etang, who is said to have been a friend of Marie Antoinette, emigrated at the Revolution and somehow drifted to India. It was, I believe, from Mrs. Pattle that the beauty of the daughters was inherited. Mrs. Cameron showed least of it; but Mrs. Jackson and Lady Somers were remarkable in that respect. The Jacksons had three daughters, besides a son who died in infancy. The daughters were Adeline, born 14 November 1837, who married Henry Halford Vaughan in 1856; Mary, born 30 December 1841, who married Herbert Fisher in 1862; and my (and our) Julia Prinsep who was born 7 February 1846. Dr. Jackson made a modest fortune in India. Mrs. Jackson returned to England with Julia in 1848 (the others were already with the Prinseps). She lived in various places, especially the Well Walk at Hampstead from 1851 to 1855; and was rejoined by Dr. Jackson in 1855. They lived at Brent Lodge, Hendon, from that time until 1866 when they settled at a pleasant house called Saxonbury, in Frant, near Tunbridge Wells. It was a good country house with a pleasant garden and two or three fields, on the top of a hill from which you looked over Eridge Park away to Crowborough and Ashdown Forest in one direction and could, in another, see the more distant Leith Hill.

So much for external facts. I will now say of Dr. Jackson that he was a worthy and eminently respectable person. He was regarded at Calcutta as a good physician, but did not practice in England. His only public appearance was at the famous trial of the poisoner Palmer, when he was called as a witness to prove that tetanus sometimes occurred in India without wounds or poison. He was not a man of any great mark: and I may tell you that I was rather puzzled, especially in the early years of my acquaintance with the Jacksons, by his position in the family. Somehow he did not seem to count—as fathers generally count in their families. Mrs. Jackson was passionately devoted to her children and was, beyond all doubt, a thoroughly good wife. But I could not perceive that she was romantic as a wife. The old doctor was respected or esteemed rather than ardently loved—or so I fancied. And this was the more obvious because of the strength of the other family affections. Certainly of all Julia's relations he was the one whom she regarded with the calmest affection. She seemed to have an incomparably stronger feeling about her mother. This may have been partly due to the fact that Dr. Jackson had never had a day's illness in his life and that therefore her instincts, so often excited by suffering, had not, in his case, been called into activity. But I think that it was due to his comparatively uninteresting character and to her not having acquired the filial sentiment (or to his not having acquired the paternal sentiment) generated by early familiarity. In her earliest years she had been brought into the closest intimacy with other relations—and especially with her uncle H. T. Prinsep, of whom I must presently speak. He was a man of altogether higher stamp and for him Julia had a specially warm devotion. I, of course, do not mean that the excellent doctor was at all neglected. He went his own way, had his little business occupations, was duly consulted as to all family arrangements: but was somehow a bit of an outsider. I shall just put down a small anecdote which amused me. Once, when Mrs. Jackson was ill in Calcutta, she was attended by a Dr. Rankin who declined to take a fee from the wife of a colleague. To show her gratitude, she bought a pretty watch for him. Meanwhile Rankin had hit upon the preposterous notion of converting Dr. Jackson to agnosticism. The excellent doctor, who went to church as regularly as to his dinner, altogether declined to argue the point. Rankin thereupon declared that he would have no intercourse with a man so deaf to the calls of reason; and further sent back the watch, by way of symbolically shaking the dust off his shoes. Years afterwards, when I was Julia's husband, Rankin turned up in London—I don't know what his intermediate adventures had been—very poor and very ill. Dr. Jackson went to see him and did what he could to soothe his last days. I went too, as Rankin had written to me about some of my articles. He died very soon afterwards, and is buried at Kensal Green, just outside consecrated ground, with a queer inscription on his tombstone— I often look at it—saying that he was 'neither theist nor atheist'. The watch meanwhile remained in a kind of limbo of suspense. Upon his death, Mrs. Jackson made it over to me; and I still wear it. When I am dead, let it go to the one who is most in want of a watch. There was a grotesque absurdity about the attempt to convert Dr. Jackson—who would as soon have visited his patients in his shirtsleeves as have resigned his

Thirty-nine Articles. But I feel a sort of kindness for poor old Rankin.

Well, I must go back a step. Mrs. Jackson's two eldest daughters were married before she left Hendon. While living there, if not previously, she had made a good many friends of some literary and artistic note. One of the closest was Coventry Patmore, known to her during his first wife's life, before he had gone over to Rome, and a friend of hers till death. Another friend was Robert W. Mackay (1803–82, author of *Progress of the Intellect*, see *Dicty. of Nat. Biog.*) an amiable and modest and, I believe, a learned man, whose friendship she also preserved. Some letters from these and others are in the large box, where I have put her letters to Julia. The others included Philip Worsley (elder brother of George's and Thoby's schoolmaster, G.T.) whose version of the Odyssey has been greatly admired; and especially Woolner, the sculptor, and Holman Hunt. Both of them admired—as how could they fail to admire? —her beautiful daughter Julia. I find from letters that about 1861–2 Woolner asked leave to make busts from the daughters (J. and M., I suppose) and that Mrs. Jackson declined on the ground that their simplicity might be injured by the implied homage to their beauty. Both Woolner and Hunt felt a more than artistic admiration for Julia and made offers. Holman Hunt seems from a letter written soon after his rejection (1864) to have taken it in a good spirit. He was a friend to the last. In 1872 he writes from Jerusalem asking Julia (then in her widowhood) to be godmother to one of his children. He says in it that he regards her with 'reverence'. His second wife has been a very good friend. I may add that Woolner and Hunt married two sisters and that Hunt's marriage of a third sister, upon the death of his first wife, led to a quarrel between them. I used to be told, though obviously such reports are not to be taken as worth anything, that these two were attracted to the said sisters by their likeness to Julia. Probably this was a conjecture of some ingenious person; but it is true, though to me not very intelligible, that the present Mrs. Holman Hunt and Julia were not unfrequently taken for each other. However, I am becoming gossippy if not scandalous. I only wished to say that Julia's beauty was conspicuous from her childhood and that as she grew up she was admired by all who had eyes to see.

Mary Fisher tells me of the attention which she always attracted in public places; and Julia speaks to me in one of her letters of Mrs. Jackson's 'superstition' that every man who met her in a railway carriage fell in love with her. I fancy that Mrs. Jackson's superstition had a good deal to say for itself.

At this time Henry Thoby Prinsep was living in Little Holland House, a quaint old-fashioned building like a rambling farm-house, with queer additions and alterations by successive occupants, which had a country air, although suburban London was beginning to threaten it. There was a good-sized garden, with a croquet ground and quaint trees. The house was pulled down, when the lease expired about 1874, and several of the houses in what is now Melbury Road occupy its place. 'Uncle Thoby' was a very noble old man—a grand specimen of the Indian official of the days of the Company. He had retired before Julia was first brought to England and he was afterwards a member of the Indian Council. (His life was written for the dictionary by Sir A. J. Arbuthnot, though it is not yet published; and quite recently Julia gave Arbuthnot information for the purpose.) Uncle Thoby became blind or nearly blind towards the end of his life. He was beloved and petted by various nieces, but above all by my darling. His wife, 'Aunt Sara' had a fair share of the family beauty, but was not very strong in respect of literary tastes. She was great at curries and cookery, fond of domestic management and proud of her three big sons—Henry Thoby, now judge of the high court at Calcutta, Arthur the soldier and Val the artist. She was a kind motherly woman in her little circle. The Prinseps took Burne-Jones into their house, when he was very ill and as yet poor and unknown. Julia always said that they saved his life; and he had always shown becoming gratitude. They were equally good to G. F. Watts who was at this time domiciled in Little Holland House. His studios were a set of quaint rooms on the upper floor. George Meredith was another friend, who often speaks enthusiastically of Uncle Thoby. *The Shaving of Shagpat* was, I believe, partly the result of some of Prinsep's oriental discourses. You see, therefore, that the Prinseps had claims upon the respect of artistic and literary people. My impression is that they did not go out into society. I think that Uncle Thoby's infirmities made it inconvenient for him, although the infirmities certainly did not affect his mental powers. But their house had a character of its own. People used to go there on Sunday afternoons; they had tea and strawberries and cream, and played croquet and strolled about the old-fashioned garden, or were allowed to go to Watts's studio and admire his pictures. I went there pretty often—after my marriage to Minny, I take it—and used, I must confess, to feel very shy. It was silly enough, for the Prinseps were both kindly and homely people. But I have always been shy with artistic people, who inhabit a world very unfamiliar to me: and then there used to be Leighton, now Sir Frederick, in all his glory; and Val Prinsep and his friends, who looked terribly smart to me; and Mrs. Sartoris, who had been Adelaide Kemble, who like the rest of her family was alarming and could talk music and the drama and other mysteries. I was, as I say, silly: for the parties were really far less alarming than those at the Leweses, where one had to be ready to discuss metaphysics or the principles of aesthetic philosophy, and to be presented to George Eliot and offer an acceptable worship. No doubt the good people at Little Holland House were about as much afraid of me as I was of them. Julia had lived in the house as a little child, and was, of course, one of the very innermost circle. Her cousins as well as Uncle Thoby made much of her and were proud of her beauty. Thackeray, as was natural, had been intimate at the house. Aunt Sara, after his death, was very affectionate to his daughters (I remember how she superintended my Minny's wedding dress!) and they made friends with Julia.

And now I come nearer to my darling's story. I do not know certainly when I saw her first: but the first time at which I remember to have seen her was at that picnic of 1866 of which I have already spoken. I remember standing on the little green before the inn at Abinger Hatch. I was talking to Jeanie Senior—sister of Tom Hughes—one of the sweetest and best of women, who, for reasons, had a kindness for me.* Julia was

---

* I must just give the reason. Her younger brother 'Harry' Hughes was my pupil at Cambridge. He was an athletic youth and died very young through breaking a blood-vessel by some over-exertion. I preached a sermon upon his death, which pleased his family. I gave them a copy which may conceivably exist. If so it is unique: for I burnt all my other sermons. Harry was just the model of Tom Brown, only simpler: he was most lovable; morally admirable; and though he could only pass examinations by

standing near us among a little group of girls. 'What do you think of Julia Jackson?' asked Mrs. Senior. I forget the words of my reply, but the substance was, she is the most beautiful girl I ever saw. My sister tells me that she was impressed at the same time and place and remembers that Julia was in white with blue flowers in her hat. I do not remember that I spoke to her. I saw and remembered her, as I might have seen and remembered the Sistine Madonna or any other presentation of superlative beauty.*

I must dwell a little more upon her beauty: for beauty, as it seems to me, was of the very essence of her nature. I have never seen—I have no expectation that I ever shall see—anyone whose outward appearance might be described as so absolutely faultless. Her portrait was very often drawn and painted by various people. She was a model to Burne-Jones for his picture of the Annunciation (belonging, I think, to Lord Carlisle). Watts drew a chalk head of her as a little child, which belonged to her mother and was left by mother to me. It is charming and

* Another instance of the impression made by her in early days is given in these verses by Sir Henry Taylor, who met Garibaldi at Tennyson's house in the Isle of Wight in April 1864. Julia was also there. I copy the poem from (I think) Taylor's own handwriting.

Something betwixt a pasture and a park
Saved from sea-breezes by a hump of down
Tossed bluebells in the face of April, dark
With fitful frown.

And there was he, that gentle hero, who
By virtue and by strength of his right arm,
Dethroned an unjust King, and then withdrew
To tend his farm.

To whom came forth a mighty man of song,
Whose deep-mouthed music rolls thro' all the land
Voices of many rivers, rich or strong,
Or sweet or grand.

I turned from bard and patriot, like some churl
Senseless to powers that hold the world in fee
How is it that the face of one fair girl
Is more to me?

heroic efforts, seemed to me to be like a man of genius whose brains had been permanently muddled by a shock. In that he was not quite unlike his elder brother. Jeanie Senior was always grateful to me for recognizing her brother's merits in spite of his troubles with examiners.

obviously like. He certainly painted two others; one was exhibited at the Grafton Gallery in 1894, and she disliked it so much that I did not go to see it. We have another Watts, which was given to me (returned to me, she said) by Mary Fisher after my darling's death. I am truly grateful to her for it and am glad to have it; but I cannot say that it commends itself to me as a conceivable likeness of her, even in her girlhood. Marochetti took her for a model, when she was fourteen or fifteen* for a monument to the Princess Elizabeth, Charles I's daughter, at Carisbrooke. He also made a bust at the same time, which has, I suspect, no great artistic merit but which does apparently give an impression of her appearance at the time. Of later portraits—one by Clifford done for Gerald, one by Lisa Stillman, etc.—I can only say that to me they appear to be complete failures. The portraits fail, I think, because her beauty depended upon an exquisite delicacy of line and form such as I never saw approached and which would have required singular felicity and skill in drawing to represent adequately. Most fortunately, the beautiful series of portraits taken by Mrs. Cameron, chiefly, I think, from 1866 to 1875, remain to give an impression to her children of what she really was. To us, who remember her distinctly, they recall her like nothing else. There are some later ones, little snap-photographs taken by Georgy and Stella and a photograph by Henry Cameron with Virginia on her lap, which touch me even more. It is possibly that I may be able to read into them something which would not be equally visible to others who have not my associations. Her features were absolutely faultless. But when I look at that photograph with Virginia I at least see a mouth which is an embodiment of such delicacy and tenderness as makes my heart tremble. This I must try to say. Her beauty was of the kind which seems to imply—as it most certainly did accompany—equal beauty of soul, refinement, nobility and tenderness of character; and which yet did not imply, as some beauty called 'spiritual' may seem to do, any lack of 'material' beauty. It was just the perfect balance, the harmony of mind and body which made me feel when I looked at her the kind of pleasure which I suppose a keen artistic sense to derive from a masterpiece of Greek sculpture.

* Not more than ten, I find, for the monument was erected in 1856: see D.N.B.

It was the complete reconciliation and fulfilment of all conditions of feminine beauty. Wordsworth expresses something of what I am trying to say, in the verses 'She was a phantom of delight' which have become a little threadbare from quotation. If you read them you will see my meaning, which is summed up in the last lines,

A perfect woman, nobly planned
To warn, to comfort and command:
And yet a spirit still, and bright
With something of angelic light!

Her loveliness thrills me to the core, whenever I call up the vision. May it never grow weaker till my power of mental vision weakens—as it must so soon.

I need hardly tell you that even in the full bloom of her youthful beauty she was as unconscious as an infant or rather as free from vanity. Her mother's judicious care no doubt helped to protect her simplicity. She knew, of course, that she was a beauty; she could hardly avoid seeing so much in her glass, and in the eyes of everyone who looked at her, and there was clearly no want of admirers to put the truth into words. But nobody could have been more absolutely unspoilt and untouched by the slightest weakness of self-complacency. As she grew older she would often assure me that she had lost any good looks that she had ever possessed, and that I was silly for denying it: I do not think that she would have wished me to be less 'silly'. Even to me, indeed, it could not be doubtful that lines of care and thought had been drawing themselves upon her face; and some grey hairs—she speaks of them in early letters to me—appeared before our marriage. But she had the rare beauty which in some ways even improves by age. If the bloom had passed away, if sorrow and anxiety had left their traces, the traces, too, became stronger of the love, the tenderness, the dignity and nobility of character which were only strengthened by the many trials of after life. She always seemed to me to be beautiful all through, beautiful in soul as in body: and I must now try to give a little more distinct impression of that inward beauty and to show that the outward form was but its fitting symbol and embodiment. Ah! my darlings, try to fix her picture in your minds. To see her as she was is to me to feel all that is holy and all that is endearing in human affection.

Now I must first go back to some circumstances of her early life. In some ways it is hard for me to speak; and yet it is the greatest solace to me to speak now. Her sisters, as I have said, married in 1856 and 1862. From that time she was the cherished jewel of her mother's home. Mrs. Jackson suffered a good deal (from about 1856, I think) from rheumatism, and Julia accompanied her to various places to which she went in search of health: St. Moritz, Aigle, Malvern and elsewhere. Julia used to tell me that Adeline Vaughan was in some ways the closest of the children to her mother's heart: not more, I take it however, than is often true in the sense of the eldest child. The marriages of the two elder daughters, however, threw the principal care of nursing upon Julia; and from an early age— she was sixteen in 1862—she was beginning to be familiar with the duty of soothing a sick-bed. Between her and her mother there grew up a specially tender relation; a love such as exceeded the ordinary love of mother and daughter and which became of the utmost importance to both of them. Mary Fisher, as she tells me, visited Venice during her honeymoon in 1862. There Herbert Fisher was taken ill, and the Jacksons joined them at Venice in consequence. Here Julia for the first time met Herbert Duckworth. He was then a young barrister, taking a vacation abroad, and was a friend of Herbert Fisher.

I must now say a few words about Duckworth. He was born 19 May 1833, the son of William Duckworth who at some later time (I do not know the precise dates) bought Orchard Leigh, near Frome, where his son Arthur still lives. Herbert Duckworth was at Eton and afterwards at Trinity College, Cambridge, where he took his degree in 1855. He was called to the bar and joined the Northern Circuit. I knew something of him at Cambridge. His cousin Frank Coleman was one of a little set to which I belonged in my undergraduate days (it included F. V. Hawkins, Howard Elphinstone, W. F. Robinson and Henry and Edward Dicey); and we met, I seem to remember, at Coleman's rooms. Only one little picture remains distinct in my mind, which I will describe for the sake of the suggestion conveyed. I had a cousin, G. B. Atkinson, a very good fellow, but given, as I thought, to a rather excessive admiration of the outward and visible signs of gentleman-like breeding. He was at my college and looked up a little to me as a person of intellectual claims, but thought me scandalously slovenly in dress and altogether wanting in the true social polish. At the beginning of term I wanted to meet Atkinson and after writing and seeking him in vain met him in Trinity Street. 'Why did you not come to see me?' I said reproachfully. He explained that he had paid his first respects to H. Duckworth and his evident conviction that Duckworth had the first claim upon his allegiance caused me a sharp pang of jealousy. He explained to me, then or at some other time, that Duckworth was his ideal, the perfect type of the public school man, whereas he took me— as I inferred—for a sort of Diogenes, an unworldly (in a bad sense) and intellectual person. He must have vexed me or I should not have remembered the incident so clearly. It was, I suppose, an early indication to me of the light in which the awkward slovenly student appears to the man of sense and taste. Herbert Duckworth, in all seriousness, was not only a thorough gentleman in the best sense of the phrase, but had the outward indications of the character which may be valued a little too warmly by men like Atkinson, but which have a real value. He was good at fives (as I happen to remember) and at other games, without being excessively devoted to athletic pursuits: he was capable of passing examinations creditably, though he did not aim at distinction in the Senate House, and altogether was the kind of man who might be expected to settle down as a thorough country gentleman with all the very real merits that belong to the character. A man of honour, of fair accomplishments and interest in books, he was fitted to take his place in any society, without being the least of a dandy or a fop: simple, straightforward and manly. But, besides this, he was, as everyone could perceive who knew him, a singularly modest and sweet-tempered man. I think that the sweetness of temper was perhaps his most obvious characteristic. I vividly remember his smile, for I often see it on the face of his son George. I might have spared any attempt at description by saying to you, my dear George, and to your brothers and sisters, that you are strikingly like you father. I think that he was a little heavier of build and slower of mind, but the likeness is unmistakeable; and I need not say more to prove that he was lovable—lovable to a very marked degree. I will just add that on circuit he became very intimate with Gully, who has just been elected

Speaker, and with Herschell, the Lord Chancellor: he had perhaps known Gully at Cambridge. For both of them your mother always retained a most friendly feeling.

After the first meeting at Venice, Julia met Herbert Duckworth again, especially, I seem to remember, in the course of some of her wanderings with her mother—in Switzerland, it seems to me, on the lake of Lucerne, and I presume elsewhere. Of all this, however, I know nothing or next to nothing. In these dark days, I have looked through a number of letters and papers referring to him from his early schooldays till the time of his death—I have placed them together in a box and there you, my children, may, if you please, look into them.

I felt—you will understand why I felt—that it was hardly right for me to examine too closely records—so tender and intimate as some of them were—of my Julia's first love. Yet I could not quite refrain. I looked into them: I was deeply moved by what I read; and I will tell you frankly what impression they made upon me. I have, however, nothing to say of the letters relating to your father's early life. I do not know that there is anything to be said about them, though as far as they went they seemed to give a pleasant picture.

I have told you that I was engaged to Minny in December 1866. I was dining with her and her sister soon afterwards, when Val Prinsep was one of the party. He announced to us the news of Julia Jackson's engagement to Herbert Duckworth. It was a very interesting announcement, as she was a friend of Anny and Minny. I remember too how Edward Dicey, who was also there, agreed with me in pronouncing Herbert Duckworth to be a very fortunate man. I cannot be sure that we did not pronounce him to be even more fortunate than he deserved: but if so, we were grievously mistaken. The engagement, I find, took place on 1 February 1867 and the marriage was from Saxonbury on 4 May following—a little before my own marriage to Minny.

Now I will say what I feel it right to say of the letters which I have mentioned. They impressed me deeply, as I have said: and a kind of fascination forced me to glance through them. There was a touch of pain—I cannot deny it—in the clear consciousness which they produced that my darling Julia had owed her purest happiness to another man. Yet as I read,

I learnt to be simply thankful that she had enjoyed such unqualified happiness for alas! so brief a period. No one, she told me long afterwards, had tasted more perfect happiness: and from everything that I have heard—from what Mrs. Jackson and Mary Fisher, for example, have told me—I am sure that this was not only true, but so true as to be evident to all who loved her. The reasons are not far to seek. My Julia took, as she would afterwards tell me, a view of marriage differing from that which is commonly held. It was in fact a view which could only be accepted by a woman of intense and exalted feeling. When she expressed what she felt, one was inclined to say 'that strain I heard was of a higher mood'. It was impossible for her to accept such a relation in any light-hearted or careless spirit, such as is common enough among thoughtless girls. Even at this early period she took life gravely, I think, and with a certain sense of responsibility. A girl of twenty or twenty-one can hardly realize all that is implied in the marriage union: and there is often something alarming in the sight of a noble and pure minded young woman accepting a husband with complete confidence—well or ill founded—in his worthiness. Julia always felt instinctively—and her letters during her engagement show her feeling clearly—that a woman ought either to refuse a man unconditionally or to accept him absolutely and unreservedly. She made a complete surrender of herself in the fullest sense: she would have no reserves from her lover, and confesses her entire devotion to him in the most simple and explicit words. 'Surrender' is perhaps hardly the right word, though it seems to express what I mean, unless you understand that the surrender was mutual. The two lives were to become one; there was to be no shadow of difference or discord; and she speaks in a way, the more touching from its quiet simplicity, of her entire unity with him. One might read such language used by a thoughtless or impulsive girl, interpreting it to mean a comparatively shallow feeling, and fear that it might turn out to be the prologue to a tragedy—to disillusionment and a discovery that devotion had been wasted upon an unworthy object. What I seemed to read in her letters is the opposite of this. The strength of her passion seems to be a guarantee not only for its purity but for its thorough insight. To be the object of such a love was a privilege beyond all price:

and Herbert Duckworth fully deserved it. The letters of which I speak begin from the engagement. They were very rarely separated; she accompanied him upon circuit whenever she was able, and the only letters after the marriage are, I think, when for some reason she had been obliged to stay at home. There are none in 1870, and I guess that in that year they were together until the end. I cannot say how far there is anything in these letters which would impress any outsider at all in the way in which they impressed me. They necessarily turn in the main upon trivial points—little matters of business, circuit or home gossip and so forth. To me who am able to read between the lines, it was impossible not to perceive the deep underlying tenderness which strengthened as the days went on. George Herbert, the eldest child, was born 5 March 1868, and Stella on 30 May 1869; and the love of their children would bind the parents more closely together. But I need say no more. For three years and a little more Julia had, as I know from herself and from others, a full measure of the greatest happiness that can fall to the lot of a woman—and, once more, I am glad to think that it was so.

I remember very little of her in those days. I think that one little picture is all that remains. I dined with her father-in-law at Bryanston Square (where she, by the way, lived when in London). I sat next to her and talked to her about a certain letter of mine in the *Pall Mall Gazette*, signed 'a stray-sheep', in which I described the preaching of one Body, a ranting high church parson. I fear that the article was not very sympathetic—to Body: and I was the more pleased when she spoke of it with approval. I am half ashamed to notice that even this scrap owes its preservation to an author's vanity! I remember, however, afterwards another much more significant scene. In the summer of 1870, as I have said, Minny and I were staying near Kingston. We had asked a few friends to come to us for a row on the river—I loved the river in those days and made many excursions upon it. I can see now most distinctly Julia with Minna Duckworth standing at a point where the road from the railway station joined the one which follows the bank. They were looking out for Herbert Duckworth who had missed the train by which he was expected to come. Julia was evidently in a state of painful anxiety, in an anxiety, indeed, which seemed to be unreasonable. She said to me years afterwards, 'how silly you were thinking me on that occasion!' I assured her (and I hope truly, for I cannot remember now) that I had been only pitying her and suspecting that she had some cause for anxiety unknown to me. Minna Duckworth, who remembers the occasion, tells me that there was no such cause at the time. Mary Fisher, who also remembers the incident, says also that it was no more than usual—Julia, she says, was always in such a state when she was separated from her husband. She used to say to Mary, 'I could not live if I had to be separated from him as much as you have to be separated from Herbert Fisher'. (Fisher was at that time tutor to the Prince of Wales and often obliged to pass two or three months at Sandringham without his wife.) Yet I think it just possible that there may have been a reason. I find a letter (dated 19 May 1870) from Duckworth's father to Dr. Jackson. Old Mr. Duckworth says that he is anxious about his son's health, asks Dr. Jackson's opinion, and says that, if a life in London should disagree with Herbert, he is prepared to increase his allowance so that he may give up his profession, live in the country and find occupation as a magistrate.

Herbert Duckworth was in fact so far independent of his professional prospects that he scarcely devoted himself to his work in the spirit of a man who has his living to make by it. He observes in one letter that he is inclined to be penitent for caring so little for his profession, being quite content with having such a wife. Anyhow, during 1870 he showed some symptoms of ill health, though they had not excited any serious apprehensions. In September of that year, he went to Wales with Julia and paid a visit to the Vaughans, who were then settled at Upton Castle, Pembrokeshire. He was apparently quite well one Sunday; he made some little effort, gathering a fig, I believe, from a lofty bough; and this, as was afterwards supposed, caused the bursting of a previously unsuspected abscess. He felt a pain after a short time, became rapidly worse, and died in twenty-four hours (19 September 1870). The blow to Julia was stunning. She was expecting her confinement, and Gerald was born within six weeks of his father's death (29 October 1870).

My darling had to pass through the valley of the shadow of

death. I have said enough to show what the blow must have
been. Life—alas! I know the feeling too well—becomes under
such trials a dream, a futile procession of images which seem
to have in them no real life or meaning: the only real world is
the world of intense gnawing pain which may be gradually
dulled, but which refuses to admit any of the brighter realities
from outside. The world was darker for her thenceforward;
for confidence was destroyed, and the very springs of life were
weakened. I can best tell what happened to her by quoting
from a letter written to me long afterwards when she had long
been in a calmer state:

'You see, dear' (she says, before our marriage), 'though I don't
feel as if life had been hard or as if I had not a great deal in it,
still it has been different from yours and from most people's. I
was only 24 when it all seemed a shipwreck, and I knew that I
had to live on and on, and the only thing to be done was to be
as cheerful as I could and do as much as I could and think as
little. And so I got deadened. I had all along felt that if it had
been possible for me to be myself, it would have been better for
me individually; and that I could have got more real life out of
the wreck if I had broken down more. But there was Baby to be
thought of and everyone around me urging me to keep up, and
I could never be alone which sometimes was such torture. So
that by degrees I felt that though I was more cheerful and
content than most people, I was more changed.'

I must explain the purpose of this letter hereafter. I will only
say now that she adds that she has told me more of herself
than she had ever told anyone. I am glad to read of her conviction that she had gained cheerfulness. But even the cheerfulness was mingled with much sadness. She became a kind of
sister of mercy. Whenever there was trouble, death or illness
in her family, the first thing was to send for Julia, whether to
comfort survivors or to nurse the patients. She became a
thoroughly skilful nurse—most tender, skilful and judicious.
She at once took command in the sick-room, and her little book
Notes from Sickrooms (1883) gives some of her experience. To be
nursed by her, I know it alas!, was a luxury even in the midst of
suffering. Yet she could not go through all these scenes without
acquiring a melancholy view of life. She says to me in a letter
of about the same date, 'Sometimes I have felt not unlike your

sister (as reported by me) that the world was clothed in drab but that it was all shrouded in a crape-veil.' She is grateful therefore to people for being happy, for 'one is 'read 'I am'?) always being called upon to sympathize in troubles'. She argues with sweet sophistry that I am more 'tender' than she, because I can try to sympathize with the happy whereas she puts them 'on a sort of mental shelf when they are bright again'. When she had saved a life from the deep waters, that is, she sought at once for another person to rescue, whereas I went off to take a glass with the escaped. Ah! my darling, I will not argue with you! It seemed to me at the time that she had accepted sorrow as her lifelong partner. She was, of course, devoted to her children; but I think that the cloud was not altogether withdrawn even in her relations to them. Gerald was delicate as was to be expected from the circumstances of his birth, and his health caused occasional anxiety. George's brightness was an immense blessing from those early days and a specially close relation sprang up between him and 'his own darling mother' as he always called her in his letters. And yet the gloom was there. She was in the state of mind which sends some women to convents, and tells me in another letter that she took a convent life to be the happiest. Once before she had told me that she always felt that death would be the greatest boon that could be bestowed upon her. It is not possible to say how far such thoughts, to which I must refer again presently, implied abiding sadness: though I take them to be rather the reflections which occurred to her when at moments she turned from her occupations and thought of the painful scenes which intervened too often between calm periods. I cannot doubt at any rate that her loving care of her children, her mother and her many friends brought her much deep and quiet happiness, though she hardly rose to brightness or to anything that could deserve a stronger name than cheerfulness. She was, as she says, 'deadened': shock had benumbed her. But I will say no more of this here.

I cannot give you any details of her kind actions at this time. I know that she nursed her father-in-law, Mr. Duckworth, in his last illness and her 'Aunt Loo', Mrs. Bayley, who died after long suffering at the house where the Leo Maxses now live.

Among Julia's best friends at this time was Anny Thackeray.

'What Anny has been to me', she says, 'I should find it difficult to describe. When I was very much alone, the children quite small, and every day seemed a fresh burthen, she used to come; and though I could never pour out, and she never talked about myself or my feelings, she somehow took me into her life; and by making me take a sort of indirect interest in things she did and people she saw, helped me into some sort of shelter and made things more real to me again.' For that, as for much else, I shall always be grateful to Anny. I remember how Julia, among other occupations, used to help Anny in her work, copy and arrange her disorderly manuscripts and so forth. I remember too that Julia used to be at Freshwater, where we occasionally went in those days. The ladies used to be engaged in the cult of Tennyson, who was occasionally well scolded for his little vanities by excellent Mrs. Cameron. Mrs. Cameron resembled Anny in impulsiveness and enthusiasm and they had an ardent friendship. Julia, too, loved her Aunt; and it was at this period that Mrs. Cameron took the photographs which best preserve the memory of my beloved's exquisite beauty.

I have told you how I saw Julia upon the eve of Minny's death. On the next day she came and I remember how tenderly she kissed me and asked me whether I had kept many letters— the only sources of comfort I could have.* Anny, I remember too, characteristically thought Julia's manner a little too restrained. Anny would prefer greater 'outpouring'. But both Anny and I were grateful when she went with us a few days later to Brighton, took a lodging close by us, and did all she could to soothe us in our sorrow. Her first concern was no doubt for Anny; for although I had already learnt to admire and respect her, she fancied still, quite erroneously, that I was bored by her, or, rather, I take it, that I was generally contemptuous towards all but eminent authors. I must have been a brute, indeed, had I not recognized her kindness.

Anny and I returned to London. We then lived at 8 Southwell Gardens. We had left our old house in Onslow Gardens in the spring of 1873, and bought the other before it was finished: so that Minny had the opportunity, in which she much delighted,

---

* My Minny's letters and mine to her are in the wooden box on my mantelpiece in the study—made from a bit of old Trinity Hall panelling.

of arranging the house internally. I thing that the close association with plans so soon to be made useless gave me a kind of dislike to the house, which, moreover, was rather large for Anny and me; and it happened that just at this time No. 20 Hyde Park Gate (then 11 Hyde Park Gate South) was at our disposal. It was part of the property of Anny and Minny. Julia had shortly before left Redcliffe Gardens, where she had lived during the previous years, to come into the house where I am now writing—22 H.P.G. (then 13 H.P.G.S.). One advantage of taking No. 20 would therefore be that Julia would be almost our next-door neighbour. We decided to make the change: and I remember how Julia managed to take us all into this house during the process of migration; and how kind John Field, one of my American friends, helped to arrange my books in the study during some oppressively hot weather and how Julia supplied us with cooling drinks to facilitate the performance. It is a trifling memory enough; but it is just one instance of the little bits of thoughtful kindness which she was always delighted to bestow.

At this time, a time, I need hardly say, of deep melancholy to me, some of Anny's friends thought, not unnaturally perhaps, that I was wanting in consideration for Anny. Her old and affectionate, though not very judicious friend, Mrs. Brookfield, reproved me for worrying Anny about money matters. I was able, as I have intimated, to make a very simple statement of facts which sufficiently showed that I was not substantially to blame upon that head. I cannot say with equal confidence that I was not occasionally irritable upon details and I find that I made a 'scene' soon afterwards when Anny brought me some unexpected bills. Julia spoke to me more to the purpose about my want of temper, as we met each other one day; and I took a turn with her in Kensington Gardens, when I had the sense to confess my shortcomings and make promises of amendment. She, I could see, was pleased at my willingness to listen to reason, and we became, I think, better friends from that day.

Here I must speak of another trouble closely connected with this. My poor little Laura was now dependent upon me. She had a German nurse, one Louise Meineke, who had been with us from nearly the first. She was, I fancy, a silly woman enough; but in my helplessness I naturally trusted her a good deal, as she had been trusted by my Minny. I must add that up to this time neither Minny nor Anny nor I had perceived that Laura was anything but a normal, though she was obviously a backward child. I can remember, though they are too sacred to repeat, little words of Laura's mother which prove to me conclusively that no suspicion of any worse incapacity had entered her mind. I am happy to remember them, for the maternal blindness saved her from a cruel pang. I find too from letters from Julia, for some time after this, believed that Laura would grow up to be like other children. As you know, such hopes were destined to be cruelly disappointed—Laura has remained mentally deficient. Now, as I began to attend to her more carefully, I became aware that she would require special treatment; and some of my remarks in the next year show that I had some dim forebodings of the truth, though I was long able to dismiss them as due to morbid anxiety. This state of things led to difficulties between Anny and me. It seems that I trusted Louise too much and practically encouraged her to resist Anny's authority. I can remember one occasion upon which Julia told me that I was acting improperly to Anny in this way. Julia's advice naturally was of great value to me, and she helped to keep things straight. She gave her opinions frankly, although I think that she considered, unlike some of my friends, that the blame did not lie exclusively with me. Indeed, I must say that I was on substantially brotherlike and affectionate terms with Anny: I never, as I find myself saying, had a quarrel with her which lasted from lunch till dinner-time: but I fancy that in the absence of Minny's gentle mediation, our occasional 'scenes' became more painful.

In the summer of 1876 Anny and I went to Coniston to be near my friend Victor Marshall. Anny, of course, made a conquest of Ruskin. I find a letter of mine to Julia written upon the back of a letter from Anny, in which I express a hope that she can interpret my growls as not meaning ingratitude. Another of about the same time thanks her very warmly for her lesson in the art of making one's own suffering useful to others. After leaving Coniston, we took lodgings at Seaford, where the Fishers then lived, and where Julia, still under the impression of my being bored by her, kept away when I was expected at the house. And now a fresh domestic trial came upon me, which had consequences. Anny had always been on the most affectionate terms with her cousins, the Ritchies. Blanche (Mrs. Cornish) and Augusta (Mrs. Freshfield) were already married, but five children still lived with their mother. Anny went abroad with a large party of them in the autumn of 1874. Reports came back that they had complained of her goings on with Richmond Ritchie. He was then, I think, between school and college. (He took his degree in 1878.) There were, it seemed, ominous symptoms of a love affair! Minny treated such rumours as nonsense and as rather unpleasant nonsense, due to the gossipping propensities of the Ritchies, and was rather indignant and quite incredulous. Now, however, Richmond was constantly at our house, and it began to appear that there was something in it. He was frequently too with Julia, of whom he made a confidant, and who showed him the sympathy which she was always inclined to bestow upon youthful lovers. At last the catastrophe occurred. To speak plainly, I came into the drawing-room and found Richmond kissing Anny. I told her at once that she ought to make up her mind one way or other: for it was quite plain that as things were going, there could be only one result. She did, I think, make up her mind and inform me of her engagement that afternoon. As Anny was, I think, seventeen years older than Richmond, it was clear that a long engagement would be very undesirable. She could not afford to waste time. Soon afterwards I read in the paper that there was to be a competition for certain public offices. I wrote to Richmond, suggesting that this was a good chance for obtaining something to marry upon. He entered accordingly and won a clerkship in the India Office. The engagement took place, I believe, in January 1877 and the marriage on the 2 August following.

Now for all this I was blamed by the whole Ritchie family—and most unjustly! They fancied that I had brought about or at least precipitated the match by asking Richmond 'his intentions'; whereas I had only spoken to Anny when speaking was forced upon me. They complained of me for ruining his degree by suggesting the public office: though if he had neglected the chance the marriage might have been indefinitely postponed greatly to Anny's injury. The fact was that if they hated the marriage, I positively loathed it. I could not speak of it to Julia without exploding in denunciations. Though my feeling was unreasonable, I am not clear that it was unnatural nor (to confess the truth) am I sure that all traces of it have even yet disappeared. I hated it perhaps, as Julia suggested to me, partly because all men are jealous and I might feel that I was being put at a lower level in Anny's affections; I certainly thought that it would make a widening gulf between us; I hated it because men at least always hate a marriage between a young man and a much older woman; and I hated it because the most obvious result would be the breaking up of my own household. I knew very little of and cared very little for Richmond. Well, it all seems absurd now. The marriage, as Julia foretold, has been a very happy one; and, as she said, one ought to be glad of anything that increases happiness. Indeed, I thought myself that she was right in her anticipation, provided only—what then seemed doubtful—that Anny should keep her health. For a time, however, the whole affair was a torture to me. I had to fight the Ritchies in a cause which I felt to be far more distasteful to me than to them. I remember how I complained to Fitzjames and how he brought down his sledge-hammer upon poor Frank Cornish who was one of my antagonists. Well, the Ritchies ended by listening to reason. They gave their blessing to the pair and the marriage came off. I told Julia that she would be doing me one of her many good services if she could succeed in reconciling me to Anny and Richmond—I mean, in removing my prejudices, for of course there was no other reconciliation needed. She did her best: but it was years before my feeling vanished, if, indeed, it ever quite vanished.

To me meanwhile there came the prospect that I should be left in solitude with Laura. But soon after Anny's engagement an event happened to which I owe all my future happiness. Ever since Minny's death, since Julia had tried to help Anny and me through our troubles, and especially since we had become next-door neighbours, had been meeting constantly, and discussing the various perplexities I have described, I had been coming to recognize more clearly the enormous value of her friendship, to perceive the singular nobility of her character, and to depend more and more upon her judgement. I have already said that she found me alarming. I appear to some people, I believe, to be silent, cold and sarcastic. It is common enough for a shy 'skinless' man—and that I certainly am—to make such an impression, especially if it is supposed that he could say something sharp if he pleased. Julia fancied that she bored me; and writing two years later observes that she had this feeling—for the last time, I hope—when I returned from my first winter expedition to the Alps.* That, I presume, must have been at the end of January 1877. She had however discovered that something less repulsive was concealed by my alarming outside. This is sufficiently clear from what I am about to tell. I was walking into town one day past Knightsbridge barracks when I suddenly said to myself, 'I am in love with Julia!' It came upon me as a flash of revelation. I had felt the blow of my Minny's death as I could not but feel it. It had, for a time, crushed me. All hope all but vanished from my life. Yet the 'all but' meant a good deal. I can remember how even at the darkest period I said to myself, 'Some day something like happiness will return'. In fact my sorrow, deep and genuine as it was, had not, so to speak, injured me organically. There are sorrows which permanently weaken the very power to be happy; others which, deep as may be the gloom which they cause, do not injure the capacity for happiness but only deprive it for the time of its sustenance. I had still a power of reaction. And in this respect, no doubt, there is a difference between the masculine and the feminine way of taking life. Julia, as I have said, had been numbed and petrified by her grief: womanlike she had accepted sorrow, a life of sorrow, or let me say a life clouded by sorrow, as her permanent portion. I though plunged into deep melancholy always resented or resisted the thought of a complete abandonment of the hope, at least, of happiness. I still somewhere, deep down in my nature, was able to carry on a struggle against the dominion of grief. And so it came to pass that by this time, that is the beginning of 1877, I was capable once more of a strange feeling of—what shall I call it?— of something like joy and revival. It seemed again that there was a music running through me, not altogether cheerful, very far from altogether unhesitating, but yet delicious and inspiring. Julia was that strange solemn music to which my whole nature seemed to be set. The music has made all my

* See 'Winter in the Alps' in the *Playground*, last edition.

later life a harmony till now. Can I still live in the strength which it has given?

I cannot say whether I really struggled at all: certainly I did not struggle long against the desire which now came to me to be once more comparatively happy. It happened—I don't remember why—that John Ball (of the *Alpine Guide*) and his wife proposed to dine with me. (Ball, a very amiable and accomplished man, was well known to me through our common love of the Alps, and had been my neighbour at Southwell Gardens.) Anny happened to be away: probably engaged with Richmond? I asked Julia to dine with us. The dinner itself has vanished from my memory. The Balls left and as Julia was following them, I gave her a note which I had written that day. It is now in the box with all my darling's letters, and I have copied it with two or three which followed into my extracts. I told her that I loved her as a man loves the woman he would marry. I told her that I knew that she had no such love for me. I had, therefore, no hope of being her lover, though there was nothing which I more ardently desired than to be her friend. I promised 'on my honour' that I would never speak of love again. Why, then, speak at all? Because I could not help it and because her unsuspecting sweetness made me love her more and more. Yet I could not cease to see her without apparent ingratitude. I did not see how to escape without her help. I told her, therefore, that I would do without a murmur whatever she wished. I would cease to see her as we were seeing each other; or I would continue to see her (I admitted that I should prefer this) if she could trust me, and hoped that when we had this mutual understanding, I should be able to subside into the appropriate frame of mind.

She took my note with a little glance of surprise which dwells with me. I was just about to go to my study when there came a knock at the door. My darling had read the letter and had instantly returned on the impulse of the moment. She went with me to my study and there we had a talk which, though I have not retained the precise words, can never be forgotten. I remember how she patted my shoulder tenderly and caressingly, and told me that I had rightly divined her feelings. Our marriage, she said, was out of the question: but she could trust me and we were not to go further apart. We were for the future to be on terms of the closest friendship: but never upon closer terms.

This happened on 5 February 1877. I can fix the date from my letter, which says that it is Monday (confirmed by two following letters). Monday that year was the 5th. For some reason my darling thought that it was on the second; and always reminded me, who invariably forget dates, upon succeeding anniversaries—for the last time on 2 February 1895.

During the following year we saw each other constantly, whenever we were both in town or at the same place in the country. We were separated, however, for a few weeks and during these periods wrote to each other daily, sometimes oftener. The letters happily for me are nearly all preserved, and, in order to make intelligible what I shall have to say of them, I will first set down the dates of our partings. I went to Brighton, alone with Laura, at the end of March and stayed there and at the Huths' near Haywards Heath a fortnight. She went to Saxonbury. I went over from Brighton one day to spend two or three hours with her. She visited the Fishers at Seaford a day or two later; and I walked to Lewes, where she had to wait an hour for a train, and spent the time walking with her and Georgy (who was quite unconscious of anything odd!) up to the old castle. At the end of June, I was for a few days at Skindle's hotel, Maidenhead; I was out of sorts, partly, I think, from vexation at Anny's marriage and attendant worries, and she came to Maidenhead on my last day, with Georgy, when we took young Herbert Fisher, then at a neighbouring school, for a row on the river, remembered both by him and by Georgy. In July I went to Coniston with my sister and Laura. I came up to town alone to be present at Anny's marriage from my house (2 August) and returned to Coniston on the 3rd. On 22 August I went to stay at Saxonbury. Julia had already in April explained matters to her mother, and I was consequently received as an intimate friend. I afterwards took lodgings at Frant, where I was joined by my sister, and stayed there till 30 September, when I walked to Bromley (the walk is described in one of my letters) and returned to London. Finally at Christmas I went again to Brighton, while Julia went to Saxonbury and to Seaford. There is much mention in these letters of John Morley and of George Smith, both of whom then lived at Brighton and were very friendly. But neither of them asked me to dinner on Christmas Day, which, for the first and till now the last time in my life, I consumed in solitude. I felt very lonely—no wonder!

And now I shall speak of the letters written at this period, which are an authentic record of the most interesting part of my life, and which will enable me to tell you how I came to break that promise about never speaking of love; and, what is of much more importance, will enable me to set before you the character of your darling mother. As I read them, they brought back old thoughts and emotions so vividly that I seemed to be living in the old days. During our married life, we rarely had occasion to dwell upon our mutual feelings which might be taken for granted. These letters, therefore, contain the fullest utterance of affections which—ah! I know it!—only strength-ened as the years went on. You, my darlings, may read the letters or the extracts of the most significant parts which I have copied into a book. Should you care to look at them, you will be more aware than I am that they belong to the dead past; and you will probably feel, too, that they contain a great deal of harping upon one or two themes. That is inevitable. And yet I think that you could hardly read or dip into them without loving your mother, I will not say better, but, as I say even to you elder children who know her so well, with a fuller know-ledge of one aspect of her character.

Of the letters generally I may say that from the very first hers are full of a love for me and of a confidence in me, for which I can never be too grateful. She speaks of me as truthfully, as endearingly, as if our love had been the first in both our lives. I think that any lover would have been hard indeed to satisfy who had not been entirely content with such a devotion as they express, had he been looking forward to the ordinary consum-mation of his hopes. What is characteristic of her genuine nobility is the absolute frankness with which she reveals her affection to me, although both she and I were sincerely convinced at the time that marriage was not to follow. She could not be indirect or reserved with the man to whom she had devoted herself. We had become one in spirit: nothing could be sweeter, nor alas! shall I ever again know anything half so sweet. I must now try to indicate what were the obstacles which kept us apart and by what steps they gradually melted away.

The letters written in April represent an early stage. She already loves me tenderly; she dreams of me and thinks of me constantly; and declares that my love is a blessing which lightens the burthen of her life. But this feeling is blended with a fear of the consequences to me. She fears that she is making me more restless: my position is a trying one; she remembers how she has herself thought of women who had men 'devoted' to them, who gave nothing and took everything. She doubts whether she ought to have acknowledged her feeling when I first spoke; and fancies that, if I had been parted from her, I might have found happiness elsewhere.* I of course remonstrated with all my eloquence against the suggestion that her affection had been or could possibly be anything but the greatest of blessings to me—whatever our relations. I only complained that I was prevented by the proprieties from seeing her as often and as freely as I desired—I put this in, I think, a rather exaggerated way while I was at Brighton, and made a proposition of a rather startling kind. I suggested that we might continue to live as we were living and yet go through a legal form of marriage, which would give me the right to be with her as much as I desired. She at once pronounced the scheme to be—as of course it was—impracticable, and gave as her 'easiest' reason for declining that she loved me too well. This, I gather, must have been the subject of our talk at Lewes. She told me, too, that it only convinced her of the depth of my affection but that it confirmed her belief that she was disturbing my life. She felt sometimes a fancy, she said, that she could wound but not heal. At the same time she spoke fully to her mother. Her mother naturally distrusted the stability of our arrangements. She thought that either I should be sacrificed or Julia persuaded to do what would be 'for the happiness of neither of us'. Julia, she says, found it hard to meet her own arguments in her mother's mouth. She saw how we must appear to a third person and begged me to reflect and if necessary

* I may just tell you, my children, that this has some reference to a hypothesis noticed occasionally in later letters from Coniston. It was thought by some people that Julia Marshall (now Mrs O'Brien) looked upon me with a favour which might develop. I cannot say that there may not have been some slight ground for this fancy, though I can say, so far as I was concerned, there never was nor could be a thought tending to anyone but my own love.

give her up. She would submit! The loving words which accomplished this profession would have made it impossible to accept, had there been otherwise a possibility. I had, I told her, come near to convincing her that her love was bad for me, and would never run such a risk again. The sight of her had at once driven away all my absurd fancies; her love had already brightened my whole life; and I would love her as long as I lived. But I would accept the position which she assigned to me and do my best to fit myself for it.

This topic gradually disappeared. We felt too much united to dwell upon any possible injuries to either. The last reference to it was at Coniston, I think, when she happened to say that she wished she could think that there was no harm in her love. 'I entreat you,' I replied, 'never again to tell me in a letter that your affection does me harm. Tell me when I am with you if you like, for then I can contradict you and have done with it. Or tell me as often as you please that you can never be my wife. That does not sting me, though of course I would rather hear the contrary. It may make me a little sad but not the least angry. But that other thing which you will say to me affects me as if you had given me your hand and put a pin in it.' This phrase became a proverb with us. We often laughed over it afterwards and she taunted me—with the kindliest and most loving of 'taunts'—for using such words.

The tone of my letter shows in fact that I could now feel at ease against any serious appeal to this argument. But though we had agreed to love, her conviction that marriage was impossible for her was still unshaken. When I came up for Anny's marriage, we must have had some talk, from which she inferred that I felt my uncertainty to be 'trying'. She wrote two letters, one apparently given to me on the spot and the other with a fuller explanation sent to me a few days later to Coniston. I have already quoted from the second the passage in which she describes the effect of her loss upon her. Both dwell upon this theme. She feels 'peaceful and sheltered' near me, but even when we are nearest has no courage for life: 'If I could be quite close to you and feel you holding me I should be so content to die. Knowing what I am, it is no temptation to me to marry you from the thought that I should make your life happier or brighter—I don't think I should. So if you want an answer, I can

only say that as I am now it would be wrong for me to marry . . .
All this sounds cold and horrid—but you know I do love you
with my whole heart—only it seems such a poor dead heart.
I cannot tell you that it can never revive, for I could not have
thought it possible that I should have felt for anyone what I
feel for you.' (This from the first letter.)

The second letter is to the same effect. She feels that she could
give herself to me entirely without reservation—'it seems to me
as if I had done so—and yet that there is a gulf between us'.
She concludes by saying that she has not accepted the impossi-
bility of a change without reflection. 'I think and think and
picture what the future might be with you, and though I
cling, instead of shrinking, to the idea of being as close to you
as can be, I cannot ever realize or face the idea of a fresh life and
fresh interests.' She has said all that is in her heart and if
I think it wiser to make any change, 'I will agree,' she says, 'my
own darling, to whatever you do.'

To this letter I replied in a way which gives me pleasure
even now. It 'soothed and pleased' me more I said than any
which I had ever received from her. She trusted me, I said, so
thoroughly that her decision seemed to be mine. The worst
thing that could happen would be that she should become my
wife and find she had been mistaken. Our likeness in sorrow was
a reason for keeping together but hardly for undertaking a new
life. She had spoken of having a 'lower standard' than mine.
To this I replied that I did not judge of people by their acquire-
ments but by themselves—a text upon which I had already
preached to her. I loved her for reasons which I knew but
would not express. 'And', I said, 'you must let me tell you that
I do and always shall feel for you something which I can only
call reverence as well as love. *Think* me silly if you please.
Don't *say* anything against yourself for I won't stand it. You
see I have not got any Saints and you must not be angry if I
put you in the place where my Saints ought to be.' She was
for very sound reasons a better saint for me than the blessed
Virgin. 'There, my own darling, I won't say any more. You
know that I will give you my life as freely as if you had an
official right to it. To live for you and make you happy is all I
want.' I proposed that we should settle down quietly and let
ourselves come to a clear understanding. 'There is no hurry!

You may think of me as I think of Troy' (my old collie) '—a nice kind loving animal who will take what I give and be thankful ... I kiss your hand, my own, and am your L.S.' I had said at an earlier time that I could keep my promise never to speak as a lover, 'that is, as I understand, that I would never ask you to change your decision'. I did not wish her to be biased by anything but her own feelings. If this were a fair interpretation of the promise, I can say that I kept it to the last. I am happy to think that I was sufficiently generous, and had sufficient trust in her, to abstain from any appeals as to my own feelings which could affect her judgement. She had sufficiently released me from my promise if it meant that I was not to speak of love. And I am glad to see that I already could say truly what I have ever since said with increasing truth and can say now more than ever, that my love was blended with reverence. She is still my saint.

I shall only add about this Coniston time that my later letters become more cheerful. My health was better, and we had reached a kind of understanding. We were to love each other without reserve and leave her to be guided by her own feelings. The only people admitted to our confidence—Mrs. Jackson and my sister*—saw perhaps more clearly than we did that the position could hardly be permanent. For a time, however, we seemed to be settling down, and the final impulse was given by later accidents. I returned to town at the end of September and began a new experiment. My sister was to keep house for me and our stay at Coniston had been partly a trial of this plan. She had tried, in particular, to take some charge of Laura, and at first with some success. But I had my doubts already. In one of my letters to Julia, I amuse myself with a remark made by Milly. She had wondered at Anny's marriage because she wondered that anyone should be willing to take the responsibility of looking after her! That was a very innocent view! But young men of twenty-three and middle-aged ladies of weak health look at things very differently. As Julia truly remarked, Milly always shrank from responsibility, and the causes were obvious. She had led a curious life. In early days when my father was professor at Haileybury she had a romantic

* I suppose that Anny knew about us also but she did not speak of the affair to me at any rate.

attachment to a student there. I do not know the details: but my impression is that he never professed love for her and that she did not even know whether he cared for her or not. She had, I think, expected another meeting when something took him suddenly to India. There, I vaguely think, he married and perhaps died. Anyhow he disappeared from her life; and she suffered so much that her health was seriously affected. She lived at home as the only inmate of the house with my father and mother, and with my mother alone after my father's death. She occupied herself a little with philanthropy, wrote an able book called *The Service of the Poor*, and had some very attached friends. But the life was singularly quiet and in after years she was greatly strained by nursing my mother. On my mother's death she completely collapsed. She had a complaint from which she still suffers and became an invalid, though making a few pathetic little attempts to turn her really great abilities to some account. She had, as I said before, taken up with the Quakers, finding something sympathetic in their quietism and semi-mystical tendencies. Another little book of hers, *Strongholds of Quakerism*, explains her views. Her attempts to rouse the Quakers to a revival of their old spirit led her to travel and to exertions which have, I fear, injured her; and she will, I suppose, be an invalid—and a very feeble invalid—as long as she lives. But even in 1877 she seemed to be broken in spirit. She had no power of reaction. She was hardly even a 'reed shaken by the wind', she was more like a reed of which every joint has been crushed and which can only float down the stream. Now Milly has loved me all her life; she has been more like a twin than a younger sister; and Julia used to say—of course affectionately—that she was altogether silly about me. Yet, as I found myself saying at the time, she was too like me to be helpful. If I put an argument in order to have it contradicted, she took it so seriously that I thought there must be something in it; if I was in doubt, she fell into utter perplexity; if I was sad, she began to weep—a performance which always came too easily to her. Consequently, though a most affectionate, she was a most depressing companion. And, then, the society which suited me would have struck her as worldly; while her friends, though very worthy and some of them very clever people, struck me as intolerably dull. So that if Anny was too exciting a companion, Milly was much at fault on the other side, and would have been a permanent strain upon spirits already low. Yet the plan was tried. Milly stayed with me in London for three weeks. Then her health broke down and her nurse and doctor carried her off to her own house in Chelsea. She begged Julia to give an eye to my household concerns. Another plan then became necessary. I talked of setting up a housekeeper; and my kind friends, the Huxleys, recommended to me a Miss Klappert, who had been, I think, a German governess in their family for some years. I discussed this, of course, with Julia; and had nearly settled upon the plan. I spoke of the final decision to Julia with a sadness resulting, as she saw, from my feeling that this would be a definitive arrangement, setting the seal, as it were, upon our separation. Then the thought came to her whether, after all, she could not make the effort to come to life again. While things were in this state, I went to Brighton for Christmas, and she again to Saxonbury and Seaford.

The letters from these places show that a change had taken place unconsciously. Although we had both come to accept our abnormal relation as though it were to be permanent, we had also been drawing closer and becoming more necessary to each other. The Klappert scheme brought the difficulty home to us. My Julia was in a state of painful indecision. She recognized now the existence of a 'possibility': yet she could not find courage to make it a reality. Old doubts came back: had she not been to blame for admitting her feelings to me? Was she not bound to keep herself for her children? She complains that whereas she had always held marriage to be a matter about which hesitation should be impossible, she was unable to decide. She went to the Fishers and felt or fancied a change in her relations to them. They were puzzled, she thought, by something in her manner. She talked to her mother and the talk, which she had dreaded, brought the comfort of tears and of hearing the matter discussed as something not dreadful. Yet her mother was afraid of the future and naturally nervous. All through, my darling told me every thought frankly; she begs me to forgive her and assures me that she alone is to blame for any bad result. I suggested to her that she was like a person reviving from drowning and that the process must be painful.

She sometimes feels, she replies, that she must let herself sink. I could do nothing but repeat my old assurances that I would in any case be content. I was like a man who had in any case made a fortune and had no right to complain if I did not make another. If she fretted about me, she would give me the only pain she could ever cause, for, said I,

I love you so
That in your sweet thoughts I would be forgot
If thinking on me so should make you love.

She thanked me most tenderly for my words and said at the end that she could never tell me how tender my letters had been to her. For that, too, I am now deeply grateful.

We returned to London, the whole question still in suspense. I went in as usual to sit with her one evening—I think the fifth of January. We talked the matter over once more and I rose to go. She was sitting in her arm-chair by the fireplace— I can see her now!—when suddenly she looked up and said 'I will be your wife and will do my best to be a good wife to you'.

All doubts vanished like a dream. She writes to me ten days later from Freshwater, where she had gone to see her uncle Thoby, 'My darling one. I feel most commonplace and quiet. The only thing I can't quite believe is that we are not married. Perhaps when I see you, you will go a little further off. Just now we seem part of each other and I feel as if it were all such an old thing that I need neither talk nor think about you!' She had yielded absolutely when she had once felt yielding to be right. More than seventeen years intervened between this and the terrible day when I lost her. Till then, she had been to me such a wife as no language can describe. We were married at Kensington Church, 26 March 1878. Not a fibre in me but thrills at the thought of all the goodness lavished upon me since that day.

Now, my darlings, I shall not try to follow the story of our married life in detail. I wish only to set before you some of the essential characteristics. As I sit here, a sad widower, hoping against hope that I may put together some maimed and imperfect life, I feel that I can hardly take a sane view of some things. Hideous morbid fancies have haunted me: fancies which I know to be utterly baseless, and which I am yet unable to disperse by an effort of will. I must live them down.* I will only say that you, my darling Stella, have helped me more than anyone. My George and Gerald have helped me too; but in grief like mine a woman can do more, and a woman who reminds me at every turn of her darling mother can give me all the comfort of which I am susceptible. How far I can recover —how far life has happiness in store for me—I know not. I am growing old: and I feel weak and broken. But this I know: I must seek for happiness—and not to seek for happiness would be cowardly, mockery as the word sounds—by trying to carry on her work, above all by maintaining the ties of affection which she wove between us and which are inexpressibly dear to me. You, my dears, may look forward. The years will, I hope, bring you happy days in which you will be able to look back with unmixed pleasure on the old memories: on the picture of your beloved mother, on her unspeakable goodness, and—how glad I am to add it!—upon your constant goodness to her. My only plain duty is to do my best to help you. I hope that I am helping you a little by trying to fix some of the memories which will, I trust, be a lifelong possession to you all.

First of all, let me say emphatically, my own darling did come to life again. She took up only too many fresh interests and duties. She lived in me, in her mother, in her children, in the many relations and friends whom she cheered and helped. The very substance of her life was woven out of her affections. The affections of course brought trials. I have often thought, in reading about Swift for example, that the saddest of all states of mind was that in which a man regrets that he has loved because his love has brought sorrow. That is 'the sin against the Holy Ghost': to blaspheme your best affections which are your Holy Ghost. No such thought ever could come to my darling. She loved and cherished her love and was grateful for having loved. Nor, whatever incidental sorrows it brought, could her love fail to be a deep and abiding happiness. When I look at certain little photographs—at one in which I am reading by her side at St. Ives with Virginia in the background, at the one by Henry Cameron with Virginia on her lap—I see as with my bodily

* In the weeks which have elapsed since this was written, I have, I hope, made a beginning: I shall if it seems right, modify some phrases which now seem to me to be too much tinged by the fancies indicated: 9 July 1895.

Leslie and Minny Stephen, 1867

Julia Duckworth

eyes the love, the holy and tender love which breathes through
those exquisite lips, and I know that the later years were a deep
strong current of calm inward happiness, and the trials, so to
speak, merely floating accidents on the surface. I remember her
intense and perpetual delight in her children. I have already
said how, during her widowhood, a cloud rested even upon her
maternal affections. Anny and I used sometimes to fancy that
she was rather stern to Stella. Once when I somehow ventured
to hint this to her she replied that she did not love the boys
better than Stella: but that Stella seemed to her more a part of
herself. The boys, I suppose, brought livelier memories of their
father: Stella, as 'part of herself', was to share something of her
own sadness. I think that after she became my own the thaw
which unlocked her other emotions helped her to thaw towards
the children. She could not love them better, but she could
abandon herself, so to speak, more unreservedly, with less tinge
of foreboding or doubt, to the natural flow of her affections.
Our own children were to her a pure delight. To see her with a
baby on her breast was a revelation, and her love grew with
their growth. Vanessa was born 30 May 1879; Julian Thoby
8 September 1880; Adeline Virginia 25 January 1882; and
Adrian Leslie 27 October 1883.*

Among my darling's papers were a great number of schoolboy
letters from George and Gerald with some from Stella in her
rare absences from home. I think that she never destroyed one
unless by accident. I have given them back to the writers. It
pleased me to find them, for every one of those letters represents
a thrill of motherly love and gratitude. They are of course
hardly worth preservation for any other reason; but they
remind me, and I hope that they will serve to remind you, how
many quiet days went by, otherwise all vanished into the dim

* Vanessa's name was of course suggested by Stella's: we had, I find, chosen it some time
before Vanessa's birth which happened to coincide precisely with the tenth anniversary
of Stella's. Julian was from Julia and Thoby from her beloved uncle. Adeline from
Adeline Vaughan, who had died the year before her niece's birth, and as Julia did not
like to use the name full of painful association, we added Virginia after Julia's aunt,
Lady Somers. Adrian came from one Adrian Scrope, a fine old regicide from whom the
Stephens claimed descent—how I don't know!—and Leslie of course from me. None
of our children were christened; I object to the ceremony and feel that it would be a
profanity in me to use it—but they have quasi-sponsors, of whom I need only say that
Lowell was Virginia's godfather.

past, which were days of quiet happiness and of sweet brooding motherly love.

Now I must touch upon certain feelings which have given me sharp pangs in my morbid state, but which must be touched. I cannot dwell upon my darling's life without mentioning them. I shall try to speak with absolute sincerity. I will not knowingly either soften or darken a shadow.

First I have said that my darling came to life, After our marriage she ceased to be numbed or 'deadened'. That is true and it is the deepest truth. Yet it is true that the years of submission to sorrow had left their mark. That was inevitable. They certainly had not destroyed the capacity for happiness. They had perhaps a little weakened it, and they had left certain clouds to pass occasionally over her mind. I wish to put this as clearly as I can. My darling appeared to some people to be at times stern: so, as I have said, she struck Anny after Minny's death. I find myself telling her in an early letter that she called me 'terrible' but that if she looked at me as I had seen her look at some people, I should sink into the earth. She asks for an explanation which, if given at all, must have been given verbally, nor can I now say to what 'people' I referred. But the phrase no doubt referred to the severity which might sometimes be suggested by her noble moral nature. Whatever her judgement of persons, and I must say again that the impression of her sweetness is so strong with me as to have obliterated any memories of 'stern' or indignant looks, her views of the world and life were tinged with sadness. She was not, like Anny, inclined to optimism. The sunlight had too long had to pass to her through that crape-veil of which she had spoken. She speaks in a letter of Thoby's infantile happiness and adds that she should say, if she did not know that I should reprove her, that he could never be so happy again. This is in one of the letters written when she had been watching the deathbed of her sister, Adeline Vaughan. The tone occurred to her naturally when she spoke of life in general. She adds in the same letter that, although she had no definite religious creed, she did believe that things were somehow right at bottom. So, perhaps, in some sense do I. Now I am, as I have said, less able than she was to resign myself to unhappiness. She seemed therefore to me at those moments to accept a view against which I always instinctively struggled. In the earlier years of our marriage, we carried on a kind of running controversy upon this point which is, of course, as I said, really beyond the reach of argument. I told her in several of my letters that I regretted her views because they seemed to me to prove that she was less happy than I could wish. No doubt every one's view of the world at large is apt to be merely the converse of their observation of their own feeling. But I am glad to think now that I was misinterpreting the facts. The truth is that, as she says, she was always being called upon to sympathize with sufferers: she had so often watched the terrible havoc made by death and had had so terrible a shock to her youthful confidence that when she made a general reflection the periods of trial impressed her more than the long intervals of monotonous peace and happiness. I have felt the same illusion in reading her letters. Most of our few separations were caused by her attendance upon some sufferer; and it would be a mistake to take the mood uppermost on such occasions as the normal or average mood. The more I think of it, the more profoundly I am convinced that the utterances against which I protested were produced by this prominence of the painful periods, not by any habitual depression. She was, indeed, habitually cheerful, full of interests and always ready to be amused. But, more than this, her life was made up of loving and spending love. Of all guarantees for true happiness there is none to be compared to the consciousness that you may have many to love and are the centre of their corresponding love and devotion. The atmosphere in which you live and the very act of breathing it is then happiness and all incidental worries and anxieties are tolerable. I have tried to reconcile myself to the sadness of some life stories by a kind of arithmetical computation. If I applied it to her, I should say that her great blow came when she was 24: but even at 24 she had alas! lived nearly half her life. Before that she had had the happiness of childhood, of which she always spoke so strongly; even in her dark days, she achieved content; and when, as she says, there came to her 'the great comfort' of her love for me and mine for her, she revived; and, I believe at the very bottom of my heart, had after our marriage a life which, though it had many troubles, was a life of deep inward peace and happiness and of many hours and seasons which, if I may venture to judge from my own participation in them, were of such rare and delightful happiness as her most lovely nature deserved and could appreciate.

Her happiness of course was not of the kind which is noisy or brilliant or conspicuous. She had withdrawn entirely from society during her widowhood: and I, too, had become a recluse. We had our little society in later years. We went out and had our parties at home. When the children grew up, she took Stella to balls, concerts and so forth, as became a good mother; and she had a considerable circle of acquaintance and many very attached friends. Neither of us cared for 'society', as it is called, very much: and I take it that our household appeared to people who did care for society, as a secluded little backwater, though to me it was not the less delicious. Julia used to be at home on Sunday afternoons; and, though we did not attempt to set up a literary or artistic 'salon', I can see her surrounded on such occasions by a very lively and pleasant group. Especially, I may say, she took the keenest possible interest in young people; she was loved and admired in return by many young friends; she was happy in watching their friendships or lovemakings; and her presence was in itself a refinement and a charm. Her courtesy was perfect—sometimes a tacit rebuke to me who find courtesy to bores a very difficult duty. The pleasantest of my memories of this kind refer to our summers, all of which were passed in Cornwall, especially to the thirteen summers (1882 to 1894) at St. Ives. There we bought the lease of Talland House: a small but roomy house, with a garden of an acre or two all up and down hill, with quaint little terraces divided by hedges of escallonia, a grape-house and kitchen-garden and a so-called 'orchard' beyond. Julia loved flowers and delighted in such gardening as was compatible with the shortness of our residences. Every corner of the house and garden is full of memories for me—I could hardly bear to look at it again, I think. We made what we called a 'lawn tennis' ground on the most level bit, where the children delighted in playing small cricket every evening. I can see my Julia strolling among her beloved flowers: sitting in the 'loo corner', a sheltered seat behind the grape-house, or the so-called 'coffee garden', where on hot days she would be shaded by the great escallonia hedge; and, still oftener, in the porch from which we used to watch the cricket.

Those words represent for me a long series of scenes of intense domestic happiness. And then there were our picnics and excursions: to the Land's End, or her especially beloved Porth-Curno, or to Gurnard's Head and Bosigran Castle. She was an admirable conductor of such expeditions, catering with unimpeachable skill in the department of provisions, and keeping everyone in good temper. The sun of those dear summer days still seems to shine for me. They are associated with some of our best friends, above all with Lowell. Lowell loved our scenery; but neither he nor anyone enjoyed it more than my Julia. I can feel her sitting by me on the rocky point which bounds Porthminster Bay, watching the seagulls in whom she delighted, or on the rocks by Knill's monument—a favourite haunt of hers and Lowell's. Ah, those days were full of happiness! I must add what was not less noteworthy. Her frank kindly ways made her many friends among the poor. She took a great liking to a poor fellow called Phillips who was terribly mangled by an accident on the railway and apparently recovered after many months' illness only to die soon afterwards. To meet such cases she got up a subscription to set up a nurse for the town, who was installed two or three years before the end, and has been exceedingly useful. Last winter we lent Talland House to Mrs. Grier, a widow friend of Milly's. She sent me some notes of Julia's work in the town, from which I will copy a few words. Mrs. Grier visited the mother of a young man who had been killed on the line. 'Mrs. Stephen', said the woman, 'often comes to see me when she is down here and she done so ever since my poor son died.' 'Ah, she is a good lady', said another, 'she came to see me because she heard a ship had gone down and was afraid my lad was in it.' Another woman pointed out her gratitude to Mrs. Grier. 'Ah, Ma'am', she said with a beaming face, 'when she heard my poor lad was ill, she came at once to see what she could do. She stayed with me and helped me to nurse him herself and got a trained nurse for him; and when she saw him lying dead, she cried over me and kissed me and comforted me, and she gave me this mantle to make me look more respectable.' 'These instances', says Mrs. Grier, 'are just one or two where the direct words occur to me; but I cannot count the times when in the small, dingy crowded quarter of St. Ives, her name was mentioned with affection and fervent gratitude. It was generally sufficient to say that I was staying at Talland House to call forth some expression of the kind.' To this I shall only add that Julia took things of this kind as so much an obvious matter of course that I was only half aware of the facts; though, of course, she spoke freely of them to me as they interested her. What she did there is one—only one—of many good things that she has left behind her.

I shall now go over a few subjects as they present themselves. I repeat once more the warning that if I have to speak of many sorrows, it is not because they occupied so large a period as because her helpfulness in sorrows made these events a conspicuous part of her life. I went to the Thoby Prinseps at Freshwater soon after our engagement. She had preceded me. I found the old man deeply interested in a new proof which he had discovered of 'Pythagoras' proposition' (Euclid 1.47). It was new to him at any rate and really sound and ingenious. Thence, I cannot conceive why, nor could I at the time, I went with my nephew Herbert Stephen for a walking tour to the Land's End. Soon after my return, Julia was summoned to Freshwater again by Uncle Thoby's illness. She wrote to me that he was still talking about his problem and was anxious for an opinion which I had promised to get from some famous mathematician. I had no copy of his solution and had to spend some hours on Saturday and Sunday morning in puzzling it out from memory. At last I succeeded, walked over to Clifford's house, got him to write a little appreciatory compliment, and sent it off by the post. Before it reached Freshwater, poor Uncle Thoby was dead. I went to the funeral there with Georgy, who will remember it. Julia had been unwell and felt the effort. It was my first experience of the way in which she had to exert herself. I shall just mention another case of the same time. There happened a terrible scandal, in consequence of which Lady Somers's daughter, Lady Henry Somerset, was separated from her husband—a blackguard. It led to various family rows: but I only mention it to say that one of the first results was the calling in of Julia to help Lady Henry. We did our best, however, to keep out of this trouble. I will just mention some letters from Mrs. Cameron about our engagement, which I find with ours, because they will explain to you how I appeared to others. Mrs. Cameron wrote from Ceylon, whither she had returned in

1875. On leaving, she said, she had said 'God bless you' to Julia. Julia had replied, her sweet blue eyes filling with tears, 'Pray only that I may soon die'. Mrs. Cameron, however, says that she had foreseen the result.* I was always by Julia, tall, wrapt in gloom, appealing for pity, and 'dazzling' her by my 'vast intellect'. Mrs. Cameron, however, had discovered that I was not like some people of vast intellect, made of 'rock or steel'. I had proved this by reciting poetry to her at Freshwater. How well I remember it—Swinburne's *Hymn to Proserpine* and *Omar Khayyám*. At Saxonbury, too, I used to recite to Mrs. Jackson and Julia, feeling rather bashful; but it possibly helped Mrs. Jackson, to see that I was not made of steel. Mrs. Cameron, I must add, was really most kindly and friendly to me. She had a little scheme of her own about Julia. Her daughter, wife of Charles Norman, had died in 1873 after fifteen years' happy marriage. Mrs. Cameron wished Julia to accept Norman, who was not only a singularly handsome but a very honourable and good man. Julia was much attached to him and, as Mary Fisher tells me, used to be half afraid that Mrs. Cameron's strong will would overcome her reluctance to marry. It was not to be; but both Julia and Norman were able to preserve the friendliest relations ever after.

Our marriage was followed by a stay at Eastnor Castle, lent for the honeymoon by the Somerses. A trifle which I remember suggests one remark. As we were walking one day in the park, I playfully pulled Julia down a little slope. Gerald, then seven years old, thought that I was in earnest and assaulted me on the spot. The explanation between us was easy. But you, my elder children, were, I think, a little impressed by the fancy that I should come between you and your mother. We know now, darlings, that the fear, if it existed, was needless. I hope that by making her happier I helped to make her happier with you. But, as I find, I was myself rather uncomfortable at the time. I speak to her once or twice about you in the letters before the marriage, but I tell her that it is the only subject upon which I do not feel able to speak to her with perfect freedom. For years afterwards I felt it to be right that she should be obviously in the first place with you: and that, even if I advised or suggested

* I find on rereading that she had not seen me with Julia, but had inferred what follows from letters stating bare facts.

anything, it should be to her and only through her to you. I think that I judged rightly and was at any rate on the safe side in not appearing to claim the rights of a real father. Of late years, I am thankful to feel, Julia and I had become so much one person that no difficulty has even occurred to me in regard to this; but I used to think it rather strange that, young as you were at the time of our marriage, the instinct of genuine father-ship did not become fully developed. I was sensible of a some-thing different in our relations. And yet, my dear ones, I love you now like a father and you have always been perfect to me. I am deeply grateful for your love.

I have been dropping into narrative, but I must now take things in a different order. I will in the first place speak of the persons whose deaths during her life brought some of her heaviest sorrows but called forth some of her most character-istic qualities. It may seem to be a melancholy scheme to mark a life by these most painful milestones. I have, however, suffi-ciently warned you against the possible illusion; and to me, I fear, the method seems only too natural. The loss of my darling is something to which no other loss can be for an instant com-pared. And yet my solitude is, I can feel, the more intense because so few of those with whom I started and upon whose sympathies I could have counted, survive to care for me. Perhaps at my age this is the common experience: but it is a bitter one.

The chief of the sad events of which I speak were as follows: Adeline Vaughan died 14 April 1881; H. Halford Vaughan, her husband, in April 1885; Dr. Jackson died 31 March 1887; and Mrs. Jackson 2 April 1892. I have also to think of the deaths of her very dear friend Mrs. Vernon Lushington on 23 January 1884; of J. R. Lowell in 1891; of my nephew James Stephen, 2 February 1892; of George Croom Robertson, 20 September 1892; and of my brother Fitzjames, 11 March 1894. By speaking a little of each of these events and of certain reflections which they will suggest, I think that I shall incidentally recall some of the most interesting parts of her life; and I shall then be able to pass to her relations to you and to myself.

I give you notice that in speaking of the Vaughans, I shall say some things which I would not say unless this were intended for you and me alone. You will of course take care not to allude to statements which might give pain to their children. Adeline

Vaughan was, as I have said, in Julia's opinion the most tenderly beloved of her mother's children. She had suffered for some years from heart disease and was taken ill at Upton Castle. Thither your mother went to nurse her in April 1881. The letters which she wrote to me from the place are, I think, the saddest that she ever wrote to me. I think that I shall be able sufficiently to explain the causes. Halford Vaughan, to whom Adeline was married, when only 18, in 1856, was then professor of history at Oxford. He did not reside there; and was at the same time, I think, clerk of assize on the South Wales Circuit. He finally resigned his professorship in 1858. The lectures which he gave at Oxford (four courses only, I think) had an astonishing reputation. Froude, Goldwin Smith, Frederic Harrison and, I think, others have spoken of them to me and agreed in ascribing to them surpassing eloquence. I will say honestly that from my recollections of what I have read (only two or three were published) I should guess that he was more of a rhetorician than of a solid historian. He was, however, a man of fine presence and, I can believe, imposing utterance. His friends supposed him to possess great philosophical abilities and he was known to be employed upon a great book upon some philosophical topic—an exposition, I rather think, of ethical principles. He resigned his professorship, left Hampstead, where he had lived and been a neighbour of the Jacksons at Hendon, and retired to Upton Castle—an old ruin, as I understand, which had been made more or less habitable—in Pembrokeshire and therefore conveniently placed for his circuit: I do not know the date. Here he lived for the remainder of his life and did his work at the assizes. I had never seen him till after my marriage to Julia. He had then become very deaf and I found it by no means easy to keep up a conversation. His old friends, Froude in particular, lamented that all his brilliance had departed. My Julia, who always disliked Froude, thought that he spoke unkindly; but I must confess that this statement at any rate seemed to me to be true. I heard nothing 'brilliant'. Julia adhered loyally to the estimate which had become traditional in her family and which had gained for him the surname 'Boodh', supposed to indicate omniscience. To me, I confess, it seemed that his abilities had to be taken on faith; and that, whatever he might once have been, he had become a curiously

wrong-headed argumentative person, and moreover intellectually smoke-dried by his long seclusion from any intercourse
with contemporaries of equal ability or familiarity with the
course of modern thought. Anyhow he had a strange story. The
manuscript of his *magnum opus* had been torn up at intervals: he
could not discover by whom, but there were, I think, suspicions
of the malignity of some half-mad servant. I cannot doubt that
he did it himself, but your mother, I could see, and doubtless
his wife, if the suspicion ever occurred to her, could not bear to
entertain the thought; and I, of course, took care not to insist
upon it. Anyhow, Vaughan, disgusted with the fate of his book,
gave up the attempt to finish it, and instead of it copied out
certain marginalia upon Shakespeare—the result of long winter
evenings there—and published three volumes of them. They
are, though I cannot stop to point it out, some of the most
singular instances of misapplied ingenuity that I ever saw.
Nobody, as Bain the bookseller told me, ever bought a copy
from him except Disraeli. They cost much money as they had
to be published at his own expense; but remonstrance was useless. He afterwards published a volume of translations of Welsh
proverbs into English verse, of which it can only be said that it
was less absurd and expensive. Fragments of the great book
remained in manuscript and I examined them after his death.
Nearly all that I read was in the nature of an attempt to write
the opening chapter, written and rewritten and written over
again; but I could not even make out what was their drift or
guess at the main purpose of the book. A few later fragments
seemed to show what I believe to have been proved by other
evidence, that he had at one time or other proceeded further;
but the result was—nothing. It is hard to imagine a more wasted
life, if, indeed, he ever had the abilities ascribed to him. His
children oddly seem to have inherited none of his morbid
qualities. Will, who was devoted to him, is a most admirable
fellow, the best type of intelligent public school man, most
affectionate and honourable. Perhaps he has inherited some
of his father's obstinacy and of the sleeplessness which in the
father indicated a morbid nervous condition. He seems, too, to
represent the case in which a person learns unselfishness by
living with a selfish man. Your mother loved him dearly and I
inherit, I hope, her good will. The daughters so far as I can see

are very good but rather commonplace girls (intellectually), take life easily and neither shared their father's tastes nor were troubled by his strange divagations.

But here were materials for a domestic tragedy. This strange, self-willed, proud recluse, absorbed in his futile studies, barely sane in one direction and yet managing all his own affairs, sensibly enough I was told, keeping everything in his hands and ruling his family autocratically, was idolized by his gentle wife, who retained her belief in the genius of the man to whom she had looked up from her marriage at an early age. She was as devoted to him as my Julia was to me. Alas! I fear that her reward was a poor one. He was not, I believe, unkind, only wayward and crotchety: but he accepted her devotion as his due, frankly regarded himself as a superior being and rarely unbent or condescended to caress her. That at least is the impression which I derive from your mother's letters at this most melancholy time. Vaughan had the selfishness which grows upon a man isolated from his intellectual peers and absorbed in a task where he has no sympathies. He must have been attractive in early days. Some early letters to Julia, written on his wedding tour, when she was only ten, show that he could be playful and affectionate to his little sister-in-law. He suffered greatly from the loss in very early years (it is mentioned in a letter of 27 April 1859) of a promising boy. Your mother often told me of his profound grief upon that occasion. But the amiability was clearly not on the surface in later life. In these letters, my darling speaks of melancholy talks with him after Adeline's death, of his impracticability and strange self-absorption, and of the sad views of life which, as he told her, he had been unwilling to mention to his wife, lest they should disturb her faith. She tells me too how he talked of Carlyle. She knew that I thought better of Carlyle's conduct than most people were thinking at the time of the *Reminiscences* and, I fancy, reported Vaughan's opinions as confirmatory of mine. I see—now at any rate—that he could hardly be expected to condemn Carlyle's behaviour to Mrs. Carlyle. His own treatment of Adeline was too much of the same kind; and even in one respect less excusable, for Mrs. Carlyle must have been more capable of taking her own part than was poor Adeline. I wrote, I see, expressing a hope that I might never fall into a similar fault by becoming absorbed in my books. My darling says that Vaughan scarcely bestowed a tender word upon his wife, though he stooped to kiss her once and called her 'my dear'. How many tender words you have given to me, she says, and how precious they are to me! Ah! how glad I am to think that this was true! I hope and believe that it continued to be true. With all my faults, I was never tempted to poor Vaughan's fault of blindness to a wife's devotion.

Vaughan himself died four years later. Happily the end was sudden and your mother not present to be tortured by such another scene; for Adeline's death had been slow and painful and my poor Julia speaks most pathetically of the dying woman's dumb appeals, when she could no longer express herself, for help which could not be given. Julia of course went to Upton to help the children through their sorrow. She ever afterwards did all she could for them. Augusta's marriage to 'Bob Croft' was not very gratifying to anybody, except, I hope, the Crofts themselves. Julia could do little beyond giving sympathy and advice, whenever they could be given. Millicent's marriage to Captain Isham this year took place from our house; and my darling, who heartily approved of it, for she was much pleased with Isham, showed the keenest interest in all the arrangements. I remember how happily she looked on the day and how warmly she spoke of the young people afterwards. I have said how much she loved Will. Her sympathy for him too was specially called out when he strained his health by attending the deathbed of his friend Moor (Thoby's schoolmaster at Clifton). Mrs. Moor has sent me a tender letter which Julia wrote to her upon the occasion. I hope that dear Will will regain his strength and keep a corner of his heart for me—for Julia's sake.

I have, I think, sufficiently accounted for the sadness which marks Julia's letters from Upton. Her sister's life sacrificed and the complete disappointment of all the ambitious hopes of Vaughan and his friends were texts for a sermon on the vanity of human wishes. She felt such things as she could not but feel them. I must add that deep as was my darling's grief, like all her grief, [it] became 'transmuted' into affection for the survivors. In regard to this phrase, I add a note. The article in my *Hours in a Library* which seems to have given most pleasure, judging from what I have heard, is one upon 'Wordsworth's Ethics'. I mention this because you will find it the fullest comment I can give upon this 'transmutation'. Grief, I have said in substance, is of all things not to be wasted. I wrote the article under the impressions produced by my Minny's death. It expresses what I then felt, and what I now feel as strongly.

I will now speak of the losses of Julia's parents. I have already tried to explain why my darling's love of her father was less pronounced than other affections. He was undoubtedly a very good-natured well-meaning old gentleman: but he had, so far as I could ever perceive, a commonplace understanding, and was a worshipper of respectability. There was nothing romantic about him and he did not excite romantic attachment in others. Nothing was more striking about Mrs. Jackson than the high strain of moral feeling which she transmitted to Julia; and one could not help feeling that the worthy old doctor was imperfectly responsive to the loftier moods. He would be more easily shocked by extravagance than roused by heroism. However, he was perfectly good-humoured and kindly, though in imperfect sympathy with the poetical and lofty aspects of things; and Julia, of course, was gentle and good to him if not exactly enthusiastic about him. His unbroken health till very near the end of his life had made any special attentions unnecessary, but she nursed him at the end with her usual devotion. I saw her with him—Will Vaughan was there too, I remember—when he was on his deathbed. I have still a picture of the scene in my mind which makes me think that even the process of dying must have had its sweetness when watched by those tender eyes. The death, if it did not of itself cause unusually acute pangs on behalf of the sufferer—one can hardly feel such pangs at the close of so long and prosperous a life—caused much trouble. Poor Mrs. Jackson—now a confirmed invalid—could not part without deep affliction from the husband of some fifty years. Her nerves broke down and Julia had to stay with her at Brighton for a time which, as I see, made me rather impatient— not, of course, that I did not recognize the imperative nature of the claim. This service to her mother, however, was only one incident, a very painful one, in a long course of nursing of which I must speak at greater length.

The early marriages of her sisters had, as I have said, left to my darling the main charge of nursing her mother. Even before her marriage to Herbert Duckworth she had spent much care and time upon that duty. During her widowhood her mother had again been her first object or her first after her children. She was constantly at Saxonbury and was always, I imagine, keeping an eye upon her mother's state of health. At that time, indeed, Mrs. Jackson, though an invalid much troubled by rheumatism and always requiring a long rest in the middle of the day, was still able to walk about. She was capable of taking pleasure in her garden. I visited her with my Minny (in 1875 I fancy) and was there again in 1876: and I picture her as a tall and graceful, though already a worn and fragile lady, taking little strolls among her flowers and presiding at her table. She had not had, I should judge, at any time quite the exquisite beauty of her daughter; but she must have had great beauty and a beauty of the same type—the type which speaks of true nobility of character. In 1879 Julia suffered a good deal after Vanessa's birth. We spent the summer at New Quay in Cornwall, where she regained strength, and she was happily quite restored in the autumn. In November or December, Mrs. Jackson was taken ill at Eastnor Castle, where she had gone to visit the Somerses. Julia, of course, was summoned to nurse her, and the illness took the form of rheumatic fever. I went to Eastnor for a day or two and remember how my darling welcomed me amidst her cares. Mrs. Jackson was by that time improving. She was taken to the Somers's house in London, where we all stayed together for a time, and thence to Brighton, where we stayed at the Fishers' house, 19 Second Avenue. (They had bought it but did not then occupy it.) It was a time of much anxiety and with the usual difficulties about nurses, etc.; but Mrs. Jackson gradually improved. She returned to Saxonbury for six weeks; but it was then given up and the Jacksons settled at Brighton, 3 Brunswick Terrace, where Dr. Jackson passed the rest of his life. Mrs. Jackson made one or two trials of foreign baths, Vichy and Wildbad, but from this time became more and more enfeebled. The disease strengthened its hold and I think that she was never again able to walk. Julia of course went often to see her mother at Brighton; we frequently took lodgings near her after our summer holiday when I was able to be away from town, and the children often stayed with 'Granny'—as we always called her. I wish only to say, however, that for the following years Julia was either actually nursing or, more generally of course, more or less superintending the nursing of her mother from a distance. Mrs. Jackson, as she became more crippled, suffered much pain to which rubbers and so forth could only give a partial alleviation. Her nerves naturally became weak and she was always anxious about her children and their children in proportion to her inability to go to them in case of need. This figure of pathetic weakness was always in my Julia's mind. They never passed a day apart without exchanging letters and the successful end of every journey had to be announced by telegrams. A number of the later letters from 'Granny' are in the box downstairs—and need not, I think, be preserved. Julia had herself destroyed most of those previous to 1887, keeping only a few of earlier date, such as those upon Adeline's death.

Mrs. Jackson was always a most touching and beautiful figure in our family. In spite of her long sufferings she had, as I like to believe and I think that I can fairly believe, a happy life on the whole. Her intense interest in her daughters and in her daughters' children provided her with constant interest and enabled her to fill up the brief spaces left between the many cares of an invalid's life. To me she was always as tender as to a real son. I recall—I can speak to you, my dears, without fearing a charge of vanity—with genuine pleasure the way in which she always spoke of my letters. I did not write often, I fear—indeed, it would hardly have been possible—but I wrote to her as much as I could as if she had been my mother. Towards the end of her life, I had found that she was rather afraid of putting us to inconvenience by an intended visit. I took, as I remember, some pains to convince her that her fears were groundless. I did not protest in direct terms which might have been suspected of intention. I told her of an improvement in my health at some length, explained how good Julia had been to me and the children, and said how rich I was in affection (alas! what I have lost since!) But no affection, I said, could be of more value than hers and I hoped to see her soon in my house. It was, I concluded, never so much a home to me as when she was in it.* I speak, I see, as if I was proud of this as a literary composition, showing how insinuation may be better than downright speech.

* I have found this letter and given it to Stella.

Perhaps I am: but at least my little artifice succeeded in showing my true feeling. I have seldom been more touched than
when my Julia told me that this letter had been placed by
'Granny' in a little box where she kept a few relics of past
affection and found there after her death. It is unspeakably
consoling to me to know that she who watched every movement
of Julia's heart confided in me as she could not have confided
had she not known that I was part of our darling's happiness.
Our 'darling of darlings' is her name in Granny's letters to me.

I, however, was comparatively a trifle. In every sorrow and
pain Mrs. Jackson turned instinctively to her daughter. I do
not believe that either of them ever said a word which could
give pain to the other. They relied continually upon each other
and hardly a day passed in which Julia did not try in some way
to lessen her mother's troubles by the most delicate and loving
attentions. In spite of all the pain that love was a blessing to
both, and, as I think of it, gives a pathetic beauty to their lives.

Mrs. Jackson came to us pretty often. I remember with
especial pleasure how she spent with us at St. Ives part of the
long hot summer of 1887. George Meredith was our neighbour
for a time. I can see them now sitting by the trees which
bordered our 'lawn tennis ground' while Meredith read some
of his poetry to mother and daughter. Whether they or anyone
quite understood them is more than I can say: but a poet (and
Meredith is a true poet at times) reading his poems is impressive,
and they received his reading in a sufficiently gratifying way.
Meredith, though he has his faults, has a good heart and no
man, I think, can better appreciate beauty both of the physical
and moral kind. In Julia's case he was fully sensitive. He never,
as he wrote to me lately, 'reverenced a woman more', and he
has said the same to others. He was, I know, perfectly sincere:
and 'reverence' is the word which comes naturally in speaking
of that perfect type of noble womanhood. I have used it before.

After her husband's death, Mrs. Jackson lived chiefly with
the Vaughans at 3 Percival Terrace, Brighton. She had a serious
access of weakness in the autumn of 1891, which gave some
alarm to Julia. Evidently her long sufferings were beginning to
sap her strength. She came to stay with us in the following
spring. She was unable to throw off an attack of illness and died
peacefully 2 April 1892. My dearest felt the blow. She seemed

to be very weak herself. Her cousin, the Duchess of Bedford, lent us a little house at Chenies, where we spent a month or so and where she gradually recovered.

Of all this I can say nothing more, or can only say this: I have never seen nor can I imagine the relation between mother and daughter more beautiful and perfect. Our 'darling of darlings' loved her mother so well that it might seem as if they had been alone together in the world. But in my Julia's heart there was room for many affections and one only seemed to strengthen the others.

I have spoken of other deaths which came to her as deep sorrows, and which yet suggest to me now rather the blessedness of the love from which the sorrow sprang.

Mrs. Lushington was a very dear friend. She stayed with us at St. Ives in the summer of 1882 or 3. To her daughter Kitty Maxse, I gave the other day some little notes showing how anxiously Julia watched the mother's last illness in January 1884. For the daughters, Julia always felt an almost maternal affection. Kitty gave me some little letters referring to her own engagement to Leo Maxse which took place at our house at St. Ives in 1890, and I read them with a glow of pleasure. They show, as clearly as anything, what keen and unalloyed delight was given to my darling from anything that promised happiness to young people, especially when she loved them, as in this case, both for their own sake and their parents'. The letters are bright, playful and enthusiastic. My Julia was of course, though with all due reserve, a bit of a matchmaker. That is to say nothing pleased her more than to encourage a match between two lovers who seemed to her to be worthy of each other and worthy of the greatest happiness of life. I shall tell you, my darlings, one little story which records perhaps her greatest triumph in this direction. I had made acquaintance with F. W. Maitland, one of the 'Sunday Tramps'—a club founded by me and F. Pollock in 1879, which for some twelve years gave me much recreation and led to some pleasant friendships. I occasionally brought Maitland to our house for a supper after our Sunday excursion. Julia at once took a liking to him which showed—not that any proof was required—how quickly she always recognized a fine character when she had the opportunity. Now Florence Fisher was perhaps her favourite niece, and had been warmly attached to her from early childhood. Florence often stayed with us and though a very coy young woman and apt to be sufficiently disdainful of the average young man, showed signs of a discriminating preference for Maitland. They were both very musical, which was one bond of attraction.* Now the growing attachment did not seem to advance with the desirable rapidity. In August 1885, I took Maitland for a short walking tour, directed towards St. Ives, and judiciously contrived that we should start from Whitley Ridge, near Brockenhurst, where the Fishers were then living in the New Forest. Somehow or other, the affair still seemed to hang fire, and Mary Fisher who saw the young people together began to be alarmed lest Florence should be throwing away her affections. After a consultation, Julia resolved to bring matters to a point. She asked Florence to stay with us, and I brought Maitland again to a Sunday supper. When he left, Julia asked him to accompany her and Florence to a concert next day. He accepted but next day came a letter declining. He could not but fancy, he said, with all due professions of modesty, that the invitation was intended to give him a chance of closer meeting with Florence. Now he had a conclusive reason for not marrying, which he did not explain, although if Julia insisted he would do so.

Julia at once sent for him and asked for his reason. He then explained that he had had sensations—thoughts of suicide and so on—which had convinced him that he was in danger of insanity. Some crude medical opinion had confirmed the fear. He had inferred, like an honourable man, that he must never marry and must avoid all entanglements. Julia at once said emphatically that she did not believe a word of it. She told him that he ought at once to set his mind at rest by consulting the best expert in London. He agreed to do so, and consulted Hughlings Jackson who assured him that the whole fear was a complete illusion: he was simply suffering from overwork. He wrote to Julia giving this agreeable piece of news, but by mistake addressed the letter wrongly (H.P. *Gardens* instead of *Gate*). We waited anxiously for the reply which did not come. Meanwhile Mary Fisher came to London in a very perturbed

---

* This reminds me that I have not said, probably because I have the misfortune to be hopelessly unmusical, that my Julia loved music with real enthusiasm and to the last found a great source of pleasure in listening to good musicians.

frame of mind on the Saturday. We, of course, had no right to
mention Maitland's secret and could only hint darkly at the
existence of some indefinite obstacle. On Sunday morning I
went to Maitland's house and left a note which brought him
back in the afternoon with his good news. The affair was then
settled in a day or two; although oddly enough, another mistake
in the address of a letter, from Mary Fisher to Maitland, which
therefore received no reply, led to a short perplexity. Maitland's
missing letter found its way ultimately to us, and Julia placed
it with two or three others in a card case which Maitland gave
her in memory of this little transaction. The marriage, as I need
not tell you, has been a thoroughly happy one, as, indeed, no
one who knew the pair could have doubted that it would be. It
is possible, of course, that it might have been accomplished
without Julia's interference at this moment. But things were at
a very critical stage, and her good sense and decision and
Maitland's honourable conduct were the immediate causes. To
her, the thought of her share in promoting it brought intense
satisfaction; and Maitland has always acknowledged most
frankly and fully the greatness of the service rendered to him.

I could speak of other love affairs in which she was deeply
interested. There are, however, some facts of which it is probably better to say nothing even to you. I may trust to your
memory for some of them. This much I may say: Stella made
an impression upon more than one young gentleman, which I
have no difficulty in understanding but which did not indicate
a corresponding impression upon her. Julia always thought and
frequently said to me that no one was better fitted than Stella
to play the part of wife and mother. She hoped, as I earnestly
hope too, that the man might in time appear to whom Stella
could give herself without hesitation. But with my Julia's
exalted views of love and marriage, shared, as I believe, by
Stella herself, it was impossible that she should approve of any
match not based upon complete devotion. No such man has
hitherto appeared, and Julia trusted implicitly to Stella's own
judgement in the matter. But there were more than one young
admirer of Stella whom Julia esteemed, and one for whom she
entertained a warm maternal affection. In all cases she felt a pity
for their disappointments which led her to show them a touching kindness and to do all she could to soothe the trouble. Such

trouble is perhaps not so bitter as some which she did her best to heal, but it seemed to appeal to her with special force. In the case of which I am more specially thinking, where there were some other causes for the feeling, she became, I think I may say, to the person concerned something even more than his own nearest relations. Her regard for several young men who had not this particular claim upon her sympathy was very warm. I will name only Arthur Davies and Walter Headlam. It showed strikingly her sympathy with the young—especially for young men who seemed to her to be not sufficiently appreciated—and it was repaid in these and other cases by a kind of chivalrous devotion, most welcome to me.

There is one other young man of whom I must say a few words for she loved him very dearly—my nephew J. K. Stephen. I have told his sad story—the story which has so sad an ending— in my life of his father. She took the very warmest interest in him and his fate. There were circumstances which brought him very constantly to our house in the last two or three years of his life. I shall never forget how one morning he came in at break-fast-time and announced to us—as though it were a simply amusing incident—how an eminent mad-doctor had told him that he was in danger of madness or death. He loved and ad-mired his aunt with all the strength of his fine generous nature; and it was touching to see how, in his most excited moods, her gentle grace and dignity commanded him absolutely. My brother's family shrank so much from any open recognition of his terrible disease that (very unadvisedly, I think) they ignored the facts even to us and told us simply to forbid him the house if he should be troublesome, as though there were no allowance to be made for him. To accept our sympathy, they seemed to think, would be to admit the truth. This was a considerable aggravation of our trouble. 'I cannot shut my door upon Jem' was Julia's constant saying, and she did her utmost—little, alas! could be done by anyone—to keep things as pleasant as might be or rather as free from needless pain. In one of her last letters, she tells me how she had been to visit Jem's grave on the anniversary of his death and adds that it was one of the losses to which she found it hardest to become reconciled.

Two or three friends, of whom I must speak, were originally friends of mine. There were the Croom Robertsons, who died of painful and lingering diseases, she on 29 May and he on 20 September 1892. If you look in his *Remains*, you will find in the biographical preface a letter in which I have recorded my affection for him. He was one of my very best friends, and I used to go for a weekly talk with him at his house. My Julia did all that she could to be of use to them. A letter from his brother Charles Robertson says that my feelings for his brother 'were on his part fully reciprocated for you and Mrs. Stephen'. 'Times without number and especially . . . on the day before his death, when I read Mrs. Stephen's letter to him, he told me something of what he owed to you both and what your love and sympathy did to help him in his last years of trial and trouble.' I should be sorry indeed if I did not value my share in this gratitude, but it reminds me that when I was trying to cheer one of my special intimates, Julia was not behindhand; while of the innumerable people whom she helped few indeed owed much to me. To Robertson I owed much intellectually as well as otherwise. There were certain other friends of mine with less claims to whom she was as kind as was possible. I think especially of poor old Wolstenholme, called 'the woolly' by you irreverent children, a man whom I had first known as a brilliant mathematician at Cambridge, whose Bohemian tastes and heterodox opinions had made a Cambridge career unadvisable, who had tried to become a hermit in Wastdale. He had emerged, married an uncongenial and rather vulgar Swiss girl, and obtained a professorship at Cooper's Hill. His four sons were badly brought up; he was despondent and dissatisfied and consoled himself with mathematics and opium. I liked him or rather was very fond of him, partly from old association and partly because feeble and faulty as he was, he was thoroughly amiable and clung to my friendship pathetically. His friends were few and his home life wretched. Julia could not help smiling at him; but she took him under her protection, encouraged him and petted him, and had him to stay every summer with us in the country. There he could at least be without his wife.

Another (female) friend is happily still living. I had known a little of W. K. Clifford, a man who was as delightful as a boy and gave a more distinct impression of possessing genius than anyone, I think, whom I ever knew. I have noticed his little service on the occasion of Uncle Thoby's last illness. Julia only just saw him, for he died the next year (3 March 1879). When his widow returned from Madeira, where he died, Julia of course went to see her. They became close friends. Mrs. Clifford is both a good and brave woman and, though to my taste a little too much immersed in the journalistic element, I cordially respect her gallantry in providing for herself and her daughters and I love her for her warmth of heart. Julia was never tired of discovering and executing little plans for helping her. At one time a physician had spoken very seriously of Gerald's health and had advised a voyage to Australia. It was arranged that he should go with Mrs. Clifford, whose daughter Ethel was also very much in need of a change of climate. Happily the voyage was found to be needless for Gerald. The fact is enough to prove Julia's confidence in her friend. We afterwards lent Talland House to her for a winter; but I could not count up Julia's innumerable kindnesses to a woman who appealed to her in so many ways. Mrs. Clifford repaid her amply by the warmest affection and few people, I think, loved my darling better. Mrs. Clifford came to see me yesterday (30 May 1895) and said one thing which I shall put down. Henry James, the novelist, who always loved Julia, was speaking of us both to Mrs. Clifford before the last fatal days. 'Good God,' he said of me, 'how that man adores her!' I require no proof of my adoration, but in my morbid state it was delightful to me to hear that I made it evident to my friends. If they could see it, did she not know it? (The phrase still comes pleasantly to me: 10 July 1895.) Mrs. Clifford told me more to the same effect, and spoke so gently and cordially and sincerely that I am full of gratitude to her.

One more friendship which came through me must be recorded, for it was one especially cherished. At the end of the two volumes of J. R. Lowell's letters, published by my dear friend C. E. Norton, you will find a letter from me. I have said nothing in it which I did not deeply feel. But I might have added one thing: namely, that one great bond between us in later years was his hearty appreciation of Julia. She was exceedingly fond of him and always abounded in little delicate attentions which he tried to repay by his sweet affectionate ways. It is a pleasant thought to me that I was the means of bringing to each of them a friendship which each, I know, reckoned among the real treasures of their lives. Lowell was, as I said, Virginia's titular godfather; he wrote a charming copy of verses to his god-daughter (which I have copied on a flysheet of his letters),* hoping that Virginia might be a true 'sample of heredity'. Julia desired all his letters to her should be kept by Virginia, *not* for publication. I have put them in a box, which my daughter must carefully preserve. My longest separation from Julia was when I went to pay a farewell visit (as I felt too plainly that it would be) to Lowell in his American home. She was willing to part with me for such a purpose; but I shall never forget her sweet greeting when she met me at St. Erth on my return. I will only add that the memorial erected to Lowell in the Westminster Chapter House (1893) was entirely due to her. She made me write a letter to *The Times* proposing it—rather in spite of my own opinion; and she took a chief part in the rather troublesome negotiations which finally succeeded. Lady Lyttelton, a great friend of Lowell, helped; but Julia did more than anyone. I like to remember this friendship and to recall the warmth with which she always spoke of him.

I have I think, mentioned her warmest friends, though many other names occur to me. I could not mention half the people to whom she rendered services. My darling was always making her rounds—more alas! than her strength justified—among people whom she could help. How often I used to come home and find that she had somehow made time to carry a little comfort to someone who needed it! Besides her more serious services, she was always thinking of some little kindness. Mrs. Green (the historical writer) tells me of a little present that she has preserved, because Julia brought it thinking that it might be useful on a journey. Mrs. Green was not a specially close friend but Julia was always on the lookout for kindnesses to be done. She kept in mind all manner of little anniversaries which justified such acts. Very few weeks can have passed without her finding opportunities. I used to laugh at her for her multitudinous recollections of birthdays of nephews, nieces and cousins, or of days for going to school or holidays and 'exeats'. She always kept an eye upon her nephews at school, and when Charles Fisher went to Westminster, for example, made it a matter of course that he should spend all his Sundays with us. One of her last acts of kindness was upon hearing that some help might be

* They are now published in his *Last Poems*, 1895

given to Hervey Fisher by a new kind of frame for his head and back. She bought one and sent it, trying to conceal that she was the giver. But the Fishers knew at once that it must come from her. Young Herbert Fisher tells me that he thought of her as of a second mother; Will Vaughan is equally affectionate; and indeed she never missed a chance of kindness to any nephew or niece. I confess that I grudged a little this incessant round of kindly services; they took, I thought—and I fear that I thought truly—too much labour; and yet the reward was not small, and I like to think of them now.

I do not speak as one trying to make much of trifles. I have mentioned trifles, but they were significant of much. What I seek to impress upon you is this: Wordsworth (I somehow come back often to him, when I am in sorrow) speaks in the lines upon Tintern Abbey, of

> that best portion of a good man's life
> His little nameless unremembered acts
> Of kindness and of love.

I have the happiness of knowing some people, Anny Ritchie for example, who were always spontaneously performing such acts. But I never knew anyone in whose life they played so important a part as they did in my Julia's. They were not detached accidents, done at the impulse of the moment, but were, I might almost say, parts of a system, carried out in the forethought: perhaps I might say a kind of religious practice. She was constantly preparing them: anxious (a little too anxious I used to think at times) to conceal herself or find some excuse which would make the bestowal of a present look like the payment of a debt; never brought into contact with anyone whom she liked or pitied without asking herself, what little thing can I do to give them pleasure? I, of course, had constantly to discover how she had planned and contrived to get me some little luxury or pleasure, but, in various degrees, the same zealous affection was always prompting her to help some of her numerous friends. She was, I need hardly tell you, the best of nurses, always considering and pleasuring every want of the patient. And here was the bright side of that sad view of life which I sometimes attributed to her. She thought pain so common that she was bound to seize every chance of alleviating suffering or promoting happiness. As it seems to me, she had learnt so thoroughly in her dark days of widowhood to consider herself as set apart to relieve pain and sorrow that, when no special object offered itself for her sympathy, when there was no patient to be nursed or bereaved friend to cheer, she had a stream of overflowing goodwill which forced her to look out for some channel of discharge. A child's birthday or any little occasion or present presented itself to her as a chance of adding something to the right side of the balance in the long and too often mournful account of pain and happiness. (I will add one thing which I had omitted: her invariable and judicious kindness to servants. She used to say, till quite lately, that no servant had ever voluntarily left her, except to be married. Though this ceased to be quite true, she almost always won their friendship—with good reason.)

And now, darlings, I must try to say a little of things which lay if possible still nearer to your mother's heart or at least nearer than anything except her mother's welfare. You, my elder children, know fully, and you, my younger, will remember though with less fulness of knowledge, what she was to you as a mother. The love of a mother for her children is the most beautiful thing in the world; it is sometimes the redeeming quality in characters not otherwise attractive. She was a perfect mother, a very ideal type of mother; and in her the maternal instincts were, as it seemed, but the refined essence of the love which showed its strength in every other relation of life. Yet, because you know this so well, I feel it hard to dwell upon it at length. This much I will try to say: her love of you all was an enduring and constant source of happiness to her. Never did one of you give her pain either by bad conduct or by any insensibility to her love. She never found it necessary, she said, when you were little children, to inflict punishment; she always found that she appealed to a sufficient motive by saying that if you did not attend properly to your lessons, she would not be able to teach you. I have said already how George's open temper and constant expressions of fondness for 'his own darling mother' always were a source of delight to her. She used from the first to speak of him with so evident a thrill of maternal love and pride that I sometimes feared to speak of him affectionately. My own love of him—it was quite genuine, George—would somehow not come up to the height of her devotion: what I could say would look colourless by the side of her tender words, and he seemed to be so much her peculiar property that I shrank from the appearance of claiming any right to a share of it. I do not for a moment suppose that she loved George any better than Stella or Gerald, though circumstances in the early days led her to express herself more openly and emphatically about him. Her love for her children brought of course its anxieties. Gerald's delicacy gave her most trouble, I think, when the suggestion for his voyage to Australia was made, towards the end of 1883, as I believe. There were various ailments which from time to time disturbed us, although we had not more than the usual share. It is, I should say, rather unusual that neither your mother with seven children nor your Aunt Mary with eleven should have ever had to lament the actual loss of a child by death. In later years we had our anxieties: as when Thoby, for example, allowed a playful schoolfellow to stick a knife into his femoral artery, and again took to sleepwalking in an alarming way after an attack of influenza. I will not dwell upon such things. Someone remarked to me the other day that my love of my children must bring me many anxieties. I resented the saying, which may, however, have had a harmless meaning enough. But I should always resent it, if it were meant to imply that the anxieties were to be taken as a kind of set-off against the love. The love is in itself happiness—a constant element in one's whole conscious existence; and the troubles or blessings which it may accidentally bring must be regarded as comparatively external, not like the love itself an essential part of one's nature. My darling's rather anxious temperament made her perhaps feel such troubles rather keenly, though it is also true that she had been disciplined by her sorrow to bear them patiently and calmly. She never, I am thankful to say, had to bear the pain— the worst pain a parent could suffer and the only one which could be some excuse for regretting even love—the pain of seeing a child go wrong morally or proving by conduct that her faith had been an illusion. She claimed, like other mothers, a power of judging her children impartially. I cannot say how far that claim was well founded. This I can say, that her affection was blended with motherly pride; and that I never heard her speak of you or of anything that concerned you without that glow of love which ran through her whole life. Darlings, I write this as sincerely as gratefully. I love you all for her love of you and for your love of her.

I shall just add one thing. I can not say, nor, I am sure, could she have said which of her children she loved best. Rather it was plain that she loved them all equally or that her love for any one of you became most obvious as that one happened to need it most. But, if I may say so, you must all have noticed that though a mother's love for two children may be equal, the love for one has sometimes a peculiar tenderness, caused perhaps by special need or simply from some special affinity of character. Now my dear little Adrian, as the youngest of you, will probably have the least distinct impression of his mother. To him, therefore, I shall say that she had a very marked and tender sentiment about her 'Benjamin'. There was something, I cannot define it, which gave a pathetic turn to her emotions where he was concerned. I have been much struck by a likeness, which Stella pointed out to me, between Adrian and the beautiful drawing of his mother by Watts at an early age. Perhaps this indicates some special affinity of temperament, or possibly it was that Adrian showed a special clinging to her. Anyhow, he touched a very soft place in her tender heart. She always called him her 'joy'—or by way of a quaint diminutive 'joydé'. His photographs by Henry Cameron were by her bedside and placed so that her eyes could rest upon them from her habitual seat in the drawing-room. To hear her even pronounce his name was delightful.

And now, I must return to myself for my story is involved in hers. I must say something of a rather uninteresting topic, my literary performances, for reasons which will appear. After our marriage I wrote a book (or finished it?) called *The Science of Ethics* which was published in 1882, and, good or bad, represents thoughts which had interested me a good deal. The *Cornhill Magazine* at this time was flagging, not so much, I think, because it had become worse than it had formerly been, as because for various reasons it was ceasing to be in fashion. The public wanted something 'lighter'. At the end of 1882, George Smith spoke to me of this, and it was decided that the *Magazine* should be transformed and handed over to James Payn. Payn, I may say, is a very old friend of mine; I have known him since college days, and about the end of 1874 I had introduced him to Smith. He had been dismissed from the editorship of *Chambers's Journal* and Smith was just then in want of a reader. Payn took the place which he still holds, though he has become so crippled by various diseases that he is now confined to his chair and can hardly live long. He has always been an affectionate friend, and yet I can hardly desire for his sake that a life of so much suffering should be prolonged. I gave up the *Cornhill* without much regret and at the same time agreed to undertake the editing of a Biographical Dictionary. Smith had contemplated a general biography, but upon my advice agreed to limit it to British biography. The first volume of this work appeared in January 1885, but I had been hard at work upon it for the two previous years, 1883 and 1884. It has been, I may say, a marked success in a literary sense but very much the contrary in a financial point of view. It was a very laborious and what for me in particular was much worse, a very worrying piece of work. I had to manage whole droves of contributors, most of whom were unknown to me even by name at starting; to pacify the susceptibilities of a most fretful and unreasonable race of men, the antiquaries; to detect the impostors of whom there were plenty at starting, and gradually to sift out from them the really trustworthy contributors. I had again to superintend and investigate a great quantity of wearisome and petty detail, and virtually to learn a new art, for I had never taken any special interest in the minute researches upon which the value of such a book depends; and I had to become familiar with the right mode of setting about the task and, in short, to puzzle out the whole thing for myself. I must spare one word of gratitude to Lee, who was my sub-editor from the first and whose behaviour to me was always all that I could wish. I might have foreseen something of all this: but in point of fact I did not for some time rightly measure my strength nor the demands which would be made upon it. I thought that I should have time for other employments, and moreover I had made up my mind that the dictionary would either expire in its infancy or make such a success that I should be justified in asking Smith to allow me more help and that I should so be able to confine myself to a general superintendence, with a second in command. In the year 1883 a lectureship of English literature was founded at Trinity College, Cambridge, from a bequest of W. G. Clark. Fawcett persuaded me to stand for it: he thought that it might lead to something more—to my election to a fellowship or some more permanent employment at Cambridge. Possibly that might have been the result, had it been my sole occupation. As it was, the whole thing was a blunder. I wrote twenty lectures (which my darling preserved but which are quite unfit for further use), and delivered them in the May Term of 1884. They gave satisfaction, I believe, but I felt them to be a waste of time and an excessive burthen upon my strength. I therefore resigned the lectureship. At the end of 1884 Fawcett died. He had been, and was to the end, a very dear friend of mine; although the differences between us were so great that I am inclined to think that it was only the accident of our being at the same college during the period most favourable to the formation of friendships which could have brought us so closely together. My admiration of his powers was not the less genuine and he was, I believe, all that I have said in his 'life'. I undertook to write this almost immediately after his death, and the work involved a good deal of labour in 1885. It is one of my weaknesses that I cannot work slowly; I must, if I work at all, work at high pressure. This book, therefore, with which steady labour upon the dictionary was contemporary, told upon my strength. The dictionary refused either to die or to flourish. It became a burthen and yet, as I must confess, I took a pride in it and had a kind of dogged resolution to see it through as far as I could. It is not strange that in the beginning of 1887 I felt that it was desirable to take a holiday, though it does seem strange to me now that I did not see the necessity more strongly. I went in January to see Mrs. Clifford who was passing the winter at Clarens; I spent some pleasant days at Zermatt, and after my return we all went together to Pyports, Cobham, which had been lent to us by the Lushingtons. I fancied that I was completely well but in 1888 I had a serious attack. Julia one night found me in a state of unconsciousness. I shall never forget coming to my senses with a puzzled sense of people in the room, and then the sight of her sweet face as she stooped and kissed me—ah! so tenderly. I told her afterwards, I am glad to think, how strongly that impression was stamped upon me. Some letters from Dr. Seton to Julia which I have put with ours, give an account of my state at this time. My darling did not fully reveal to me all her anxieties, though she told me the main facts. It was decided that I ought not to give up the dictionary though I was warned to be more cautious. In October 1889 I had another slighter attack, falling on the floor of the Athenaeum Library, just as I was explaining to Sir Henry Thompson, the surgeon, how completely I had recovered and what benefit I had derived from 'sulpholine' (was it?). I persevered for another year but took Lee into partnership. Vol. XXII of the dictionary (Easter 1890) has his name with mine on the title-page. This joint arrangement lasted until in 1891 I had a bad attack of influenza. I then finally resigned and Vol. XXVII (Midsummer 1891) has Lee's name alone. I will just gratify my pride as an author by saying that the volumes appeared as follows: Vol. I on 1 January 1885; Vol. V on 1 January 1886; Vol. IX, 1 January 1887; Vol. XIII, 1 January 1888; Vol. XVII, 1 January 1889; Vol. XXI, 1 January 1890; and Vol. XXV, 1 January 1891. It has since continued with great regularity. We thus, contrary to all expectation and precedent, as I believe, kept up the rate at which we had proposed to proceed. The size has increased from greater fulness of treatment. I predicted completion in fifty volumes, and if the book should be completed on the present scale, there will, I now guess, be 65. I will add, to get rid of my literary history, that I contributed many articles to the dictionary from the first until now; that, after leaving it, I took up a history of the English Utilitarians, which I laid aside in 1894 to write the life of my brother, and that I was trying to get it started again, when I was struck by this overpowering blow.

I have put all this down to make our story clear. It is plain that I was overworking. After my first collapse in 1888, I struggled on but had to drop a part of my work in 1890 and the whole in 1891. I have since, I think, recovered completely; and my recovery was undoubtedly due to my darling's unremitting care. It gives me a bitter pang to think of all the anxiety that I must have caused her, an anxiety only partially known to me at the time—partly because she thought it wise to conceal some of the facts from me and partly because she could not bear to insist upon my giving up work upon which she saw that I had set my heart. I cannot bear to go fully into this. I will say one thing. I had always been a very good sleeper. After my attack, however, a period followed of two or three years during which, although I slept, my sleep was unrefreshing. I was starting and twitching and required various narcotics. My darling always slept lightly. I could scarcely make even a slight movement without awaking her. I would sometimes awake in a fit of 'the horrors'—in a state, that is to say, of nervous excitement and misery—with the erroneous impression that I had been awake for hours and a conviction that I should not get to sleep again. She used then to put me off to sleep like a baby, and I fancy that I was seldom quite awake for long. But I fear that I must have caused her many anxious and broken nights. Oh dear! it grieves me to think of it; and yet to let you know what she was to me, I must say something of this.

I have spoken of Halford Vaughan and of Carlyle and of their wives. If I felt that I had a burthen upon my conscience like that which tortured poor Carlyle, I think that I should be almost tempted to commit suicide. I cannot, I am thankful to say, feel that. Yet neither can I feel myself to be so absolutely free from blame as I should wish to feel. I am, like my father, 'skinless': over-sensitive and nervously irritable. I am apt also to be a little absent in mind, absorbed in thoughts about my books or my writings, and occasionally paying very little attention to what is passing around me. I have so often forgotten things that have been told me, when I was more or less in this state, and declared by way of excuse that I had never been told, that it became a standing joke against me. I am inclined too to be often silent—'you don't know how silent you can be', she says in a letter—and have spent too much time in my study. At the time of my nervous depression in particular I became fidgety and troublesome in a social point of view. I am, I think, one of the most easily bored of mankind; I cannot bear long sittings with dull people and even when alone in my family I am some-times as restless as a hyena. I remember—and certainly not without compunction—how bored I was with certain guests of ours—at St. Ives, for example, when some very good friends came to be our neighbours—and how I used to plunge away into my back den and leave them, I fear, to bore Julia. All this comes back to me—trifles and things which were not quite trifles—and prevents me from saying, as I would so gladly have said, that I never gave her anxiety or caused her needless annoyance.

I will add one thing. I made over to Julia the whole management of money. She was far more competent than I in such things. I am apt to be nervous about my solvency without just cause, and I thought that matters would go more smoothly if I systematically absented myself. I do not know whether I was altogether wise. I used to be a little worried without sufficient cause when I made up our balance-sheet and some of my worry was reflected upon her. Yet I do not honestly feel that I have much in this respect to regret. I am very glad to remember that this year, when there was a certain cause for regarding a deficit as possible, I took care to show her that I was quite content, that we had enough and could retrench if retrenchment became desirable. I cannot charge myself with more than the inevitable consequences of a nervous temperament in regard to this.

This, indeed, may be said more generally. My humours and vagaries were part of my character and, though many men are far better than I, I could not become another man. This at least I can say. My irritability implied nothing worse. I loved her with my whole heart, and loved her without qualification. She knew it—as well as I know it. Never for an instant, I am quite certain, did she take my tempers and irritabilities for symptoms of any want of love or diminution of love. 'My mother says', she told me long ago, 'that you worship the ground I tread upon'; she said it with tender pleasure for she knew it to be true. After our marriage I used sometimes to complain to her that she would not say to me in so many words, 'I love you'. (She had said it often enough in her letters before, when there was a reason for saying it!) My complaint was only in play for I loved even her reticence. In truth, husband and wife, living together as we did in the most unreserved intimacy, confiding to each other every thought and feeling as it arises, do not require the language of words. In every action, in her whole conduct, she showed her love; it shone through her life; and the use of the set of words was a trifle. Proofs of her love are not wanted by you. Abundant proofs are indelibly fixed in my memory, many of them too sacred to be revealed to any human being. Indeed, I seem to wrong my darling by talking of proofs'! I have been led to speak this way only because in my morbid state, when my own shortcomings have risen up before me, I have tried to disperse them by recalling the reality. I will only say that my vivid memory of occasions upon which she happened to express

Julia and Leslie Stephen with Virginia, at Talland. 1892

Leslie and Virginia Stephen, 1902

her love directly may explain why I complained—'complained' is too strong a word—why I enticed her to deviate from her reticence. Those occasions were so delicious. Here is a trifling little anecdote which I can tell because it is trifling, and which may help to explain. She went once with Lowell and others to the Land's End in a carriage while I walked over the moors to meet them. A heavy rain made me suppose that they had turned back and, not finding them at the Inn, I walked on to Penzance. They had been at the little 'refreshment room' and we met at the railway. Julia exclaimed upon seeing me, 'I told them that you must have come: for you never fail to keep your word!' She used to smile when I told her what pleasure that little phrase had given to me. Another trifle pleases me now. We had in these last months had some little disputes, each accusing the other of sitting up too late. There was no real loss of temper: but I said to myself, it is unworthy of us to say anything which can have even a resemblance to a dispute. Next time I will reply so as to make our argument palpably playful. I did so, and felt that the only shadow of anything like discord had vanished. She would tell me sometimes that my letters were better than my words. I tried, I know, always to write so as to please her (I wish that I could see this a little more plainly in my letters now, but it was there) and I was never away from her without complaining of her absence. And oh! the delight, the exquisite delight, of my returns—the sight of her lovely eyes lighting up and her tender smile and her loving welcome to my home, the welcome that will never come again. Dears, I am irritable, touchy, nervous, reticent, but I am not 'made of steel'. I know that through it all she knew that my strongest feeling was my love of her. I think with sad pleasure that I often told her how dearly I loved her. No slightest ice of reserve ever formed between us. She was mine and I was hers absolutely; and each knew the other's heart. I grieve for any pangs that came to her through me; and yet I am convinced that our mutual love was a blessing to her, as it was an unspeakable blessing to me.

I must speak shortly of one trouble which I brought upon her. My poor Laura began to show her defects early enough. Yet her strange waywardness and inarticulate ways of thinking and speaking did not fully open my eyes, and for some time after our marriage, Julia still believed in her ultimate development.

I think that the trouble culminated about 1882, when I find some painful references to it in my letters. We afterwards tried governesses at home, and then a governess in the country, but at last she was sent to Eastwood, where she has had a very serious illness. She is apparently nearly well now; but I know not what will happen to her. I shall only say that Julia did all that affection and good sense could suggest. At times, the duty was very painful. Once when we were at St. Ives, my dear George, then a schoolboy, remonstrated with me, saying that his mother ought not to have such a task. I thanked him, I need not say, and fully agreed. I must add that in this matter I do not blame myself. I took a considerable part in teaching or trying to teach Laura. I shall never forget the shock to me, when we were at Brighton after Mrs. Jackson's illness of 1879–80, I think. We had sent Laura to a 'kindergarten' and the mistress told me that she would never learn to read. I resolved to try and succeeded in getting the poor child to read after a fashion, although I fear that I too often lost my temper and was overexacting. My darling Julia was, of course, vexed by my vexation and had her full share of the trouble; but I do not think that my conduct in the matter caused her any needless trouble.

There is another part of our relations of which I must say something. I used—as it is not very necessary to say—to take a constant pride in my noble wife. When I walked into a room with her, I used to say to myself, everybody present must see that she is the noblest person present. And she took pride in me! Alas and alas again! Did I deserve it? Does it matter whether I deserved it or not? I will try to show what, in part at least, it implied. I used often to grumble about my literary performances. In my early letters, I used, I see, to point out my inferiority to my friend John Morley and in later years I used to describe myself summarily as a 'failure'. Now, partly for my own sake, I will tell you what my view about myself really is. I know, of course, that I am a man of not inconsiderable literary ability. I think again that I am a man of greater ability than a good many much more popular authors. I have been approved by many men whose approval is worth having. When I think—as Julia would tell me that I ought to think—of the way in which my friends have spoken of me, of Lowell and Norton, Croom Robertson and H. Sidgwick, and Morley and Cotter Morison

and F. Pollock and F. W. Maitland and many others, I admit
that I ought not to complain. My darling used to tell me that I
was the most ungrateful of men for not being more pleased.
Certainly I will admit that I am not a 'failure' pure and simple;
and if my books have not sold largely, I admit that reasons may
be given, not all uncomplimentary, and that in any case failure
to win such popularity would not justify whining. The sense in
which I do take myself to be a failure is this: I have scattered
myself too much. I think that I had it in me to make something
like a real contribution to philosophical or ethical thought.
Unluckily, what with journalism and dictionary making, I have
been a jack of all trades; and instead of striking home have only
done enough to persuade friendly judges that I could have
struck. I am far indeed from thinking that this matters very
much; but I do feel that if, for example, the history of English
thought in the nineteenth century should ever be written, my
name will only be mentioned in small type and footnotes whereas, had my energies been wisely directed, I might have had the
honour of a paragraph in full sized type or even a section in a
chapter all to myself. One cause has undoubtedly been my want
of proper self-confidence or, in early days, of ambition.

Well, I state this that I may the better explain my Julia's
feeling. She used to accuse me of excessive modesty, though I
hope that she did not dislike the quality on the whole—
whatever its right name. I used sometimes I must confess (as
indeed I confessed to her) to profess a rather exaggerated self-
depreciation in order to extort some of her delicious compliments. They were delicious, for even if I could not accept her
critical judgement as correct, I could feel that it was distorted
mainly by her tender love. Although she could perceive that I
was 'fishing for a compliment' she could not find it in her heart to
refuse me. Again and again she would tell me that it was unworthy of me to complain of my want of popular success—
which, as you have seen, was not my serious complaint, though
I sometimes put it in that way. She assured me that she was a
better judge of writing, of my own writing at least, than I was.
When I retorted by declaring that she was partial, she declared
that she had liked my writings before she had known me. 'Long
ago,' she tells me when I was at Coniston, 'when I was frightened
of you and should almost have disliked you, I almost think, I

used to say to myself, he can't really be so scornful or he would not write as he does. So you need not think for a moment, darling, that I care for what you write because I care for you.' I find about the same time that she was pleased with an article of mine called 'A bye-day in the Alps' (1873 or 4?). If I had remembered this, I would have republished it in the new edition of my *Playground*. I find a copy of it, with another article or two of mine, torn out of the old *Cornhill*, which she seems to have kept, bless her! She gathered up every compliment that she thought would please me. My dear nephew, Herbert Fisher, tells me how strong during the last two years was her desire that I should have the appreciation which, she thought, was my due; how she thought that my lectures did good and were appreciated and always (as is true) encouraged me to lecture. He told her, he says, how much he admired me and how valued friends of his at Oxford, such as Alexander, thought me (I quote his words) 'one of the greatest of philosophical writers' (!) and how if they did not tell me, it was because they did not think their praise worth having. I say nothing to the compliment—except that I do not doubt H. Fisher's sincerity; but I know how much such things pleased my love and how glad she was to repeat the substance to me. In saying this, I know that I am confessing a weakness. I am so touchy that I have long ceased to read reviews of myself; even praise often worries me, and as I will not read hostile remarks I feel that I have no right to read flattering remarks. She saw some of the reviews and, I presume, despised the unfavourable. But what I wish to note is her eager interest in my performances. She read my life of my brother (which had to be typewritten) and welcomed it so warmly that she put me into good heart about it. Of late years, I have given some lectures at Ethical Societies and elsewhere. She attended almost all. The sense that she was present was delicious. When I had finished, I was generally doubtful of my success. Never shall I forget the bright glances with which she assured me that I had done well, the tender pressure of her dear hand as we went away together, and her loving declarations that I had never spoken better and that everyone was enthusiastic. The last occasion alas! was on (I think) 31 March last, when I gave two lectures. She came to both and made me thoroughly happy by her delicious praises. I had a plan for publishing some of these.

She told me that I must do so; and I half think that when I am
stronger I shall try to put them together in memory of her, with
some additions. But I must try to satisfy myself that they are not
unworthy of such a purpose.

My darling says in one of her early letters that my love of her
is as great a miracle to her as any of the miracles in which I
declined to believe. Such a sentiment is of course not uncom-
mon, and if I replied, as I could with perfect truth, that her
love of me is to me quite as marvellous, you might think that we
were both indulging in lovers' commonplaces. It is in fact
difficult, I suspect, for a woman to understand the feelings with
which a man regards her and the converse is equally true. I can
not doubt, without impugning her judgement, that there must
be somewhere something lovable in me. I will not ask what.
But the sentiment came naturally to her: for humility, in the
sense of unconsciousness of her own charms, was one of her
obvious characteristics. She thought no more of her beauty to
all appearance than if she had been as plain as—I need not
particularize. And she was equally unaware of the inner beauty
of soul. I have quoted what she said of her having a 'lower
standard' than mine; and I have given the reply which it suggested to me. This, I will add here, was in fact the natural
diffidence with which a person who acts from instinct regards
the person who acts by logic—or professes to be so guided. You,
it seems to such a one, have a theory and a rule and therefore
you must have higher principles than I. There is a fallacy in
that upon which I need not dwell. Her instincts were far more
to be trusted than my ratiocinations.

But this suggests the last remark I shall make. In one of the
letters upon our engagement, Mrs. Cameron asks, what is the
value of literary fame? Tennyson, she says, had said that a man
of genius might be lucky were he remembered for 1000 years;
and what, as the psalmist asks, is a thousand years? The commonplace is familiar in my thoughts. Had I—as I often reflect—
no pretext for calling myself a failure, had I succeeded in my
most ambitious dreams and surpassed all my contemporaries in
my own line, what should I have done? I should have written
a book or two which would have been admired by my own and
perhaps the next generation. They would have survived so long
as active forces, and a little longer in the memory of the more

learned, because they would have expressed a little better than other books thoughts which were fermenting in the minds of thousands, some abler and many little less able than myself. But putting aside the very few great names, with whom I could not in my wildest fancy compare myself, even the best thinkers become obsolete in a brief time, and turn out to have been superfluous. Putting my imaginary achievements at the best, they would have made no perceptible difference to the world. Now I say advisedly that I do not hold an achievement of that kind, and I have not even approached it, so valuable as the achievement of my darling's life. Few, indeed, except ourselves will know much of it; and when I am dead, no one will speak about it. But its value was the outpouring of a most noble and loving nature, knitting together our little circle, spreading its influence to others, making one little fragment of the race happier and better and aware of a nobler ideal. That result may be maintained and propagated. She will continue in that sense at least to live in our lives. As her dear Lowell said

> In every nobler mood
> We feel the orient of her spirit glow:
> Part of our life's unalterable good,
> Of all our saintlier aspiration.

We can preserve the ties which she formed. Her beloved nature not only soothed much suffering but was the very mainspring of the affectionate intercourse which binds us together. I cannot bear to speak of resolutions for the future, knowing how things change and how we change; but if at this time there is any aspiration deeply fixed at the very core of my heart, it is, my darlings, to carry on her work and to keep close together, always remembering her, trying to act in her spirit and to show ourselves worthy of having been her husband and children.

I cannot venture to speak of the last terrible time. No doubt her unsparing labours for us and for others had produced that weakness of the heart, of which we knew something, though not the very slightest foreboding of the reality had even crossed my mind. I thought that she had fully recovered from her influenza and even in that last week when the ominous word 'rheumatic fever' had been pronounced, I hoped against hope. When George called me on that fatal morning of the 5th of May, and I came down to see my beloved angel sinking quietly into the arms of death, I received a blow which shattered my life and has till now made the thought of happiness a mockery, but which has left me a memory that will, I can even now hope, encourage me in time to work for you.

This is 30 May: the birthday of Stella and Vanessa. I have given to Stella a chain which I gave to her mother upon our marriage; and to Vanessa a photograph by Mrs. Cameron which, as I think, shows her mother's beauty better than any other. We will cling to each other.

LESLIE STEPHEN

I finish copying this on 11 July 1895. I have made a good many alterations, as I proceeded—the most substantial changes in the account of the time between my first declaration of my love (February 1877) and our marriage. These were suggested by re-reading the letters of the time and copying many passages from them in the volume of 'Extracts'. I have altered a good many later passages, partly correcting slovenly phrases and repetitions, partly from a few letters, etc., which have since turned up, and partly adding a few thoughts which occurred to me as I read my manuscript over again. I will put the original manuscript and the 'Extracts' in a box which contains the correspondence between my own darling and me.

After this, four folios of Stephen's fair-copied manuscript consist of a chronological summary, in which he puts down 'some of the dates to which I have referred in the preceding—partly because I like to fix them in my own mind, partly because, if you ever look at the letters, you may find them convenient'. The list, from his birth on 28 November 1832 to '1895: 5 May—alas!', contains a few notes on events, scarcely any of which supplement the narrative except in closer datings. As they are available more conveniently in Maitland's Life *and elsewhere, the list is not repeated here. The only additional note worth preserving, which reflects on Julia's happy relationship with her servants, is this, under 1888: 'This year, I think, Suzette, the Swiss maid who had been with Julia since her first marriage, had an operation for cancer. She lived two or three years more and went to die with her friends at Zurich. The children's nurse, Leyden, who had been equally long with Julia made difficulties and had to leave us. But Julia befriended her and she was in this house on 5 May (1895).'*

Thereafter the method changes again, and on 8 November 1895 he records the decision that 'I propose to make a few notes in this book of anything likely to interest you hereafter'. The second part of the record continues as a mixture of a necrology with obituary notes, and a reflective journal with family information. The Mausoleum Book *concludes as follows:*

On 20 October 1895 I gave a lecture at the Ethical Society upon 'Forgotten Benefactors'. It is to appear in a forthcoming collection of lectures. I mention it because the intention was to speak of Julia without mentioning her name. The substance and sometimes (I suspect) the phrases coincide with the later part of the foregoing.

I notice that between the date of my brother's death and the publication of my life of him (little more than a year) the following had died, some his intimate friends and all men from whom I had expected information—Lord Coleridge, Lord Bowen, T. C. Sandars, C. H. Pearson and Froude. They are all mentioned in the life. Today I see announced the death of another old friend of his and mine, John Ormsby—died 30 October. He was a *Saturday* reviewer, an Alpine companion of mine, translated *Don Quixote*, and was a most kindly companion, full of humour. In later years deafness separated him from his friends; but he wrote to me very kindly last May, and I was thinking of writing to him when I heard of his death. One more link gone.

My sister has just gone to Cambridge, meaning to settle there and abandon Malvern.

James Dykes Campbell, a very good friend of mine in late years, died in June. I wrote a letter to the *Athenaeum*, giving some recollections of him. His widow has consulted me about a republication of some of his papers in the *Athenaeum* and elsewhere: but from what I see of them, I fear that I must advise against.

In the above I have omitted to speak of one of Julia's friends, Margaret Veley. She was a kind of Miss Brontë: a very clever novelist, who had been brought up in a quiet country place and developed talents scarcely appreciated by her family. She came to know me in early times of my editorship of the *Cornhill Magazine*. I accepted some contributions from her and she was grateful to excess for my approval. She was even painfully modest and shy. After my marriage to Julia she came to our house sometimes and became a warm admirer of my beloved. She attempted to draw a portrait of her as 'Mrs. Austin', the heroine of one of her novels—which is, however, no real portrait. She used to send little Christmas cards, very prettily drawn and with verses in a beautiful handwriting. After her death Julia had these framed with a photograph of Miss Veley, which you may see. I wrote a little biographical preface to a volume of Miss V.'s poems published by the mother, Mrs. Veley, after the daughter's death. There you may find a few more details.

28 January 1896. I went today for the first time to see the gravestone at Highgate. It was done for us by G. Frampton, who did Lowell's memorial. We wished for something simple: the thought of the flowers was partly suggested by the grave at Kensal Green. I think it is what we wanted.

On 25th died two links to old days: A. Macmillan, whom I knew from 1850 when he was a shopkeeper at Cambridge, and Leighton, the painter, whose dawn I remember and whom I used to see in the old days at Little Holland House. Neither were intimates but both friendly in their widely different ways.

31 January 1896. I may note that a bust of my father has just been given by my sister-in-law, Mary Stephen, to the National Portrait Gallery. It was taken by Marochetti, at my sister's desire, when my father was growing old. She disliked it so much when it was nearly finished that she persuaded my father to sit for another to Munro (a young sculptor who died soon afterwards). I have the Munro while my brother took the Marochetti. Fitzjames thought his own much the best and considered it (so Mary Stephen tells me) to be his most valuable possession. Milly and I agreed in thinking it a coarse caricature and preferred the Munro, which, though not a great work of art, is, I think, a really good likeness. My children may like to know so much of their grandfather's busts. I may add that Fitzjames's preference of the Marochetti was to my mind characteristic. It made Sir James look like the statesman dictating a despatch to suppress a rebellion, but took all the delicacy out of his face.

Fitzjames revered our father even more than I did: but could not help thinking that his sensitiveness was a weakness to be regretted. F. W. Gibbs tells me that my father said that he should wish to be known to posterity by the Marochetti. I do not think that he cared much about being 'known to posterity' or that he was a good judge of a likeness of himself. But it is worth recording the fact.

I have just been made a Trustee of the above Gallery by a coincidence.

14 March 1896. My book of Lectures mentioned on the last page has just come out. I thought of dedicating it to her, for her liking for the lectures was really the cause of their publication. I did not dedicate it, because they seemed, on reading the proofs, to be too bad. In the last, however, you will find a sufficient indication of my feeling.

Thoby has the mumps at Clifton—begun 19 March 1896.

24 March 1896. Yesterday died my old friend, Thomas Hughes, 'Tom Brown', in his seventy-third year. A younger brother of his, Henry Salisbury Hughes, was a pupil of mine at Trinity Hall. You will find a notice of him in my lecture 'Forgotten Benefactors'. Tom was very like his younger brother —a most excellent fellow with muddled brains. I used to see him off and on and he was always friendly, chiefly for the sake of Harry: but I never knew him intimately. His brother Hastings, now settled at Boston, U.S., is, I fancy, the last of the family, and like them all very amiable but not very clear in his head!

23 September 1896. We have just returned from a holiday spent at Hindhead House, Haslemere, lent to us by Mrs. Tyndall, widow of my old acquaintance: a very friendly 'acquaintance' too, enough to be called a friend. I have lately been trying to help Mrs. Tyndall to write her husband's life, i.e. giving her a little advice about it—which probably suggested to her to let us have the place.

The great event of the holidays, the greatest that has happened since our calamity, was my darling Stella's engagement to J. W. Hills on 22 August. It is superfluous to say much of this. We shall all remember all about it; and I will only note that there is an allusion to J. W. H. on p. 78. My Julia had constantly talked of the affair to me: she would have been more delighted than any of us; the thought of her approval would have reconciled me if reconciliation had been needed. But it also implies that we all knew Hills so well for so long that his adoption as one of the family makes hardly a change in our feelings about him. I cannot imagine that I could contemplate Stella's marriage with more perfect confidence and satisfaction under any conceivable circumstances. If any thing could make me happier, this ought to: but my happiness is a matter of rapidly diminishing importance.

This is so important an entry that it ought to have a page to itself. Still, I shall just note that Adrian is to begin school at Westminster tomorrow (24 September).

I don't quite like the tendency of this to become a series of obituary notices. Yet I must note that Harry Leslie Hughes was lost on the *Drummond Castle* a few months ago. He was son of my friend Hastings, brother of Thomas and Harry Salisbury, Hughes. He was born just after the death of his uncle Harry (see last page) and named after him and me. I was his godfather. Owing to Hastings Hughes's settlement in the U.S. I have seen very little of the youth; but he seems to have had an unusual share of the fine qualities which made his uncle so lovable. I note, too, that Millais died 13 August and Lady Tennyson 10 August. Both of them recall old memories: Millais I could have expected to live to a hundred, and thirty years ago Lady Tennyson seemed too frail to live a year.

And now (9 October) comes the death of G. du Maurier, whom I have known for many years and who was kind to me last summer. I told him (truly) that the first book which I could read with a certain pleasure after my loss was *Trilby*, I think because it expresses in a touching way the dwelling on old days: which is now my least painful mood. Old Mrs. Darwin, too, has just gone, who in former times received me kindly at Downe—a calm, sweet and bright old lady whom I liked because I had a special reverence for her husband.

19 October died Emelia, widow of Russell Gurney and daughter of my mother's sister, Caroline, Mrs. Batten. She is just mentioned in my life of Fitzjames. In our childhood, she was one of our most intimate circle, and I have many memories of her—not worth recording. She was a very kind, gentle

woman and after Gurney's death lived quietly and spent money on charity. She fitted up an old churchyard chapel (I think it was) in the Bayswater Road as a memorial to her husband. It was to be a kind of refuge, where people might turn in and meditate. I don't know whether much meditation is done there. She had a turn for religious novelties, a little, I think, for the Harris who humbugged Laurence Oliphant, and a desire to find some sort of mystical shelter. I fancy, too, that she thought me rather a brute as despising such things. But she was amiable when I saw her at rare intervals. My sister has kept her up, as she has kept up other members of that old circle which to me seems so quaint and old fashioned. E. Gurney's long illness had made her death desirable.

As a relief to such things, I shall just say that I put together a 'birthday book' for amusement, which has just been published by Gerald's man, Dent, as the 'bookworm's birthday book'. I am ashamed to own it and hope that my authorship will be kept a profound secret!

I am writing Sir W. Scott for the dictionary and often feel that I wish the fag end of my life to be like his—barring the debts. I must not work myself to death: but I don't know that I shall do anything better.

3 December 1896. Last week died Mrs. Brookfield, Thackeray's old friend and especially attached to A. I. Ritchie. Also Coventry Patmore, who was intimate with Mrs. Jackson when he was a young man and always a great friend of hers to the last. I never liked him, nor he, I suspect, me. But it was only a case of Dr. Fell. Why should I make these obituary notes? They remind me of much but I cannot give my recollections—they are too vague and uninteresting. Perhaps it would be better to say nothing.

10 April 1897. Today Stella was married in Kensington Church to J. W. Hills. I will not put down even here the thoughts which have agitated me. Of the marriage itself there is of course nothing to say except that it is in all respects thoroughly satisfactory. It has seemed to me as if I felt a presence all day and I know that she would have rejoiced. Alas! how much happier we should all have been! This household will be changed—for the better, let us hope, in time. Just now, my mood is to resent such assurances. The last seven or eight

months of the engagement have brought me a good many selfish pangs: but—well, I should be a brute if I really complained.

Adrian seems to be getting acclimatized at Westminster. Thoby is doing well at Clifton having waked up from some slackness due to rapid growth. I hope that he has stopped now. Virginia has been out of sorts, nervous and overgrown too; I hope that a rest will bring her round. Nessa has been hard at work at her drawing class and is, I hope, getting on well. 'Ginia is devouring books, almost faster than I like. Well, the young ones are satisfactory.

My poor Laura was settled with Dr. Corner at Brook House, Southgate, on 14th January. We had heard some complaints of Red Hill, where he had been physician, and upon his setting up this establishment thought it best to place her there. It seems to be good; but when I saw her the other day, I was pained by her looks and ways. She is unable apparently to recognize any any of us clearly.

A plan was lately started for the nurse at St. Ives. Mrs. Hain, wife of the chief man there, proposed to raise a sum to be called the Julia Prinsep Stephen fund, which would put the nursing on a permanent footing. They calculated that £300 would do this. We got some subscriptions from our friends, and as I had lately received £500 left to me by Mrs. Russell Gurney, I gave £200 to the fund. This, I hope, will make it safe and is the best memorial of my beloved.

Stella returned on Sunday 25 April from her wedding-trip. She was apparently quite well that day and on Monday. She was taken ill on Tuesday. The attack soon appeared to be peritonitis. On Thursday things looked very serious. That night, however, she improved: on Sunday the doctors admitted that she was really out of danger—and a terrible fear has been removed. She will require nursing, etc., but all looks well. I have not yet seen her.

(7 May). Two years ago!

26 June, Mrs. Oliphant died. I first met her at Grindelwald when we were staying there in the summer of 1875. She then had her two boys with her and was very bright. Now both boys are dead and before their death had given her much trouble. She was, they say, glad to die, and I don't wonder: but she was

a brave good woman and kind to us. I have not seen her for the last few years.

Stella, I note, is still laid up. She has had two relapses. The doctors, however, give good accounts of her now.

My darling Stella died early on the morning of 19 July 1897.*

24 September. We returned last night from Painswick, where we spent the holidays. We had a quiet time, with visits from one or two friends and the society, always soothing, of the Maitlands. George was with us for a month; Gerald (who spent a fortnight or so at Droitwich for his health) for about a fortnight; and both of them, with Jack, came most Sundays. I think that we are all the better for it, sad as the time has been. 'Ginia, I hope, is improving, though still nervous. I must mention here that J. W. H. offered, and I felt it right to accept his offer, to contribute to my expenses out of the income which he receives as Stella's heir. She had made no will, but, as I know, would have been desirous that this should be done to enable me to keep up this household for the good of her brothers and sisters. I mention this here, without details, because I wish you to know that J. W. H. has acted in this way; and, further, that if circumstances alter, he would be in no way bound to continue what I think he is right in doing now. Well, we must take up our work as bravely as we can.

18 February 1898. Frederick Waymouth Gibbs died this afternoon. He would have been seventy-seven if he had lived till the 27th (I think) of this month. He has been one of us since he came as a child to be in my father's house as a companion to my eldest brother, Herbert. He went to Cambridge, did well at Trinity and got a fellowship there; though he did not take honours, being prevented I believe by a severe illness—a brain-fever(?) I seem to fancy. Then he went to the bar and about 1850 became tutor to the Prince of Wales. After leaving that place, some seven years later, he went to circuit again, but never got much practice. He became a Q.C. in time and was always respected by everyone, but hardly made any particular mark. To us, he has always been a most kindly and thoughtful

* I had not the heart to say more when I wrote the words above. I read this in 1900 and will just add that the most striking thing was the singular revelation of Stella's beautiful character, when after her mother's death she had to take care of me and again when she became engaged to Jack. It did not seem as if she really changed but as if she showed her true self more clearly and brightly. Everyone near to her noticed it. Alas!

brother: not brilliant, but sensible and affectionate. He has especially been most useful to my sister, whom he helped in all business matters. His love of information and consequent cross-questioning used to bore me, and I fear, for Julia reproached me for it, that I did not always conceal the fact. But our attachment was deep and genuine; he was one of the few people whom I could trust absolutely, and with his death I become more palpably solitary.

For the last month or two my sleep has been bad. I hope that I am improving, but I note that about the end of the holidays (Christmas 1897–8) I had an attack of sleeplessness which still (4 March) holds me. I hope that I am improving but meanwhile I have cut off all work. Sometimes I doubt whether I shall ever be fit for much work again.

25 March 1898 died my old friend James Payn, born 1830. I have known him since we were at College. In later years he has been crippled by gout and rheumatism. He could not leave his chair and I used to call for a chat on Saturday afternoons. He took his pains most bravely, always cheered up when friends came, and was full of interest and goodwill. He was the best of the 'journalists', a worshipper of Dickens and not a philosopher, but really bright and lively and a gentleman. To me, again, this is a great loss, for Payn was the one friend of College days (except one or two Cambridge residents) whom I had still kept.

I am, I hope, getting my sleep back gradually—but I have had to throw aside that incubus of a book again!—and indeed all work. Poor old Thoby has had the measles at Clifton and, when he began to convalesce, a second attack. It has spoilt the term for him.

21 May 1898. Spent this Easter at Brighton. At the end of the holidays, Will Vaughan was engaged to Madge Symonds— much to my delight. She is a very sweet and very clever young woman. She was a great pet of her father and able to be an intellectual companion. Since his death, she has been much depressed and seemed reluctant to admit the idea of being happy again. All which I note, first because Will Vaughan is just the fine manly fellow to make her happy and to be happy himself, and secondly because it reminds me that this too has come about partly through Julia and Stella. Madge knew and loved Julia: she stayed with us some weeks one year, and when

Will went to Davos first one Christmas, Julia introduced him to the Symondses and had some presentiment of this. Stella often tried to promote it afterwards, and Vanessa had a share in it as an ambassador in the last period.

They were married at the beginning of the summer holidays and have set up at Clifton. During the Long Vacation, Herbert Fisher was engaged to Lettice Ilbert, daughter of Sir C. P. Ilbert, an old acquaintance of mine. Miss Ilbert took a first class at Oxford and was coached, as I hear, by H. F. She is 'highly commended' but I have not yet seen her. Not to be married till next year.

We spent the summer holidays of 1898 at Ringwood. The children, I hope, liked it and we had various people—three Rasponi children among others—to stay with us. The weather was hot and we had a long drought. The heat made me uncomfortable and my sleep was shaky; but it has since very much improved and I am setting to work again.

On 22 October F. W. Maitland, with Florence and his little girls, started for the Canaries. He got a chill at the end of June, had a bad attack of pleurisy and though he has recovered from that, is still in a state requiring absolute rest, and stay for six months in some place where he can be out of doors. I am uneasy about him, for he is the best friend I have left. Anny Ritchie has been ill all the summer with swelled glands in the neck, requiring operations and going from one bath to another. She is now at Harrogate.

Thoby goes in for an examination, in which Trinity and Trinity Hall combine, on 1st November. I am not sanguine.

11 November. Thoby got an exhibition at Trinity last night— the best piece of news I have had for a long time. His examiners have spoken very well of him. Scholarship vague, but general ability specially displayed in an essay upon 'living English poets'!

January 1899. Good reports of Maitland's health at Canary, and Anny also much improved.

My sleep quite good again—if that matters. I have had to resign my trusteeship of the National Portrait Gallery, being too deaf to be of any use at the meetings.

Went to Brighton with the children on Wednesday 12 April. Thoby joined us travelling from Clifton. On Thursday he had a very sharp attack of pneumonia. It had really begun on Monday the 10th and the doctor detained him over Tuesday and then foolishly let him start (says that he did not know of the *double* journey). Two nurses and a day of great anxiety. Things went well, however, after the first (Wednesday) and he is now (28th) quite convalescent and returned from Brighton. I had come back yesterday. The Brighton doctor thinks very decidedly that Thoby has been overdoing it. Long runs at Clifton questionable.

Maitland returned much better. Young Herbert Fisher lately engaged to Lettice Ilbert (last page), and Edmund to Jeanie Freshfield. Anny Ritchie much better: hardly quite clear yet.

3 October 1899. Today I saw Thoby off to Cambridge, to his rooms in Whewell's Court. He left Clifton on very good terms with everybody and seems to have distinguished himself chiefly as an essayist. He has been quite well, though he had a slight recurrence of his illness at Clifton. The summer spent at Warboys. Thoby weighed 13st. 8½lb. the other day—after lunch!

We spent the summer holidays of 1899 at Warboys, near Huntingdon—goodness knows why!—but all, except me, enjoyed it.

1 March 1900. I note that I had a bad attack of influenza about the end of the Christmas holidays and was completely prostrated for a time. I am only just beginning to feel decidedly convalescent. My wretched book stopped partly from this cause and partly because this terrible Boer war has stopped all book-selling. The printing was more than half done. It has ceased to interest me for the time.

Thoby is rowing in the First Trinity 4th boat.

25 March. Virginia set up the measles and is still (8 April) in her room, but has gone on well.

2 June. A giddy fit—pitched over as if I had been shot—Seton calls it 'stomachic vertigo' and seems to think little of it. Another slighter attack in July. A hint—perhaps the influenza's legacy.

The *Dictionary* finished by Vol. LXIII end of June. I had to present a testimonial to Lee and to pronounce an encomium, which he deserves. Also to propose the Lord Mayor's health at a lunch given to celebrate the completion of the book. Previously the Prince of Wales dined with Lee and I had to be present. Lee and George Smith much pleased with all the compliments they have received—I envy them the power of being pleased by such things, which to me are a weariness of the flesh.

Charles Norton over here for a flying visit as Ruskin's executor. I saw him two or three times and he was very affectionate and charming. We parted, knowing that we should never meet again.

Have promised to edit J. R. Green's letters for Mrs. Green. She ought to do it herself but I must do what she wants. I have come to think better of her. She is a singularly generous woman and a staunch friend who has been very good to me—not, as I once fancied, merely polite to the author. The death of Mary Kingsley at the Cape has upset her singularly. M. Kingsley was not only very clever—even more, a bit of a genius—but a good kind woman who is a loss to me also.

Henry Sidgwick, one of my best and oldest friends, taken ill, had a terrible operation, and has resigned his professorship. Alas! He died 28 August—and so breaks one of my last links to old Cambridge days.

30 September. We returned on the 17th from Fritham, Lyndhurst. The place was delicious: lovely forest and heaths and solitude, and the rest of the family all enjoyed themselves thoroughly. Even I enjoyed the place more than I have any place since St. Ives. For the rest, my satisfaction was rather spoilt by the recurrence of my giddy fits. They seemed to come oftener, and after returning to town I was overhauled by Ferrier. He says no organic disease (I did not suppose that there was!) but my whole state very low; to look after digestion and possibly go abroad a bit this winter. The only question, I fancy, is whether the machine is or is not too worn out to recover any vigour. (These fits have not recurred and I seem to be better. 21 April 1901.)

Gerald has been to Aix les Bains for his rheumatism. I wish he were more attentive to sanitary conditions of life.

In December, I went once more to an Alpine Club dinner, really to take Thoby with me and let him hear me speak for once in my old surroundings. I believe that I gave satisfaction. It is probably my last appearance in the old character.

April 1901. We spent a fortnight this Easter at Lyme Regis

in the Palgraves' cottage. While we were there, my old friend George Smith died (6 April). I made his acquaintance first at the end of 1864, when I was 'commencing author', wrote for him in the *Pall Mall Gazette*, edited the *Cornhill Magazine*, and, afterwards, the *Dictionary*. He was a fine generous fellow and always very friendly to me. He had his rows with some authors but was, I believe, as liberal and honest as a publisher can be. Mrs. Smith has been a model wife for near fifty years—I met Minny at their house in the early days and feel grateful for their kindness to her and to Anny. I have written a trifle in the *Cornhill*.

We could not go to Brighton this time on account of poor Mary Fisher's troubles. She is there with Adeline R. Williams nursing Hervey, who has gone off his head entirely. It seems to be very doubtful whether he will ever recover. It is a terrible blow after all these years. H. Fisher is at Lymington, whither they had all gone to save him from the winter climate of Brighton. He is, I fear, growing weaker.

Arthur Fisher came back from America with a sunstroke, and is also off his head and in an asylum. Savage reports (about 1 July) that he will get well in six months or so. The Fishers trying to let their house at Brighton and are just now at Oxford— H. F. is ordered to change on account of his health, but a rather better report of him. Emmy rather bad too and coming to stay with us (which she did not).

Harry Stephen just made an Indian judge. As he seems never to have got briefs, this is highly satisfactory. As Herbert has his clerkship and Kate and Helen are at Newnham and Manchester, the family is provided for. Rosamond and Dorothea seem to settle down as virtuous females with Anglican propensities.

Thoby has been to the 'Lake-hunt'—seeing my dear old hills.

4 October 1901. Summer holidays at Fritham again. My fits having departed, I could walk and enjoy it better. Gerald at Aix again. George after some time with us has gone with A. Chamberlain to Constantinople. I have sent Adrian to board at Westminster. Accounts of his school progress were unsatisfactory, and I hope that he may have a better chance there. His great growth—over 6ft. 2in.—has tried him.

The Fishers hardly better, if so well. Arthur in an asylum

terribly despondent, Hervey apparently less sane, though
physically better; their father, though they speak of improvement, very weak. How Mary stands it! (Arthur died not long
afterwards.)

Anny Ritchie has left Wimbledon and is settling in St.
George's Square. Her health better and Richmond seems to
have felt the railway. So they try town again.

28 December 1901. In *More Letters of Edward Fitzgerald* just
published, I find one to me (p. 277) giving an account of the
picture of a youth in scarlet, now belonging to me. E. F. bought
it from a 'poor dealer' who said that it was of Major André by
Sir Joshua. E. F. gave it to Thackeray who was then writing
The Virginians. I do not think much of the authority for the
likeness but there is some interest in the later history.

On 26 November 1901 I was made honorary D.Litt. at
Oxford; I am the same at Cambridge (1892 I think), and
LL.D. of Edinburgh and Harvard. I am honorary fellow of
Trinity Hall and foreign or corresponding (or something) mem-
ber of the American Academy, the Massachusetts Historical
Society and the American Society of Antiquaries.

Nessa—I am ashamed that I forgot to note this—got into the
Academy School last summer and has been working there
steadily since our return to town. She sent the drawing for the
Academy to a competition at her old studio, where it got the
medal. Adrian, I think, has improved by his boarding at
Tanner's.

15 January 1902. I am one of the 'original fellows' of the
British Academy for—something or other—moral and historical and philological studies, or to that effect. The thing has
hung fire.

1 February 1902. George telegraphed today from Islay that
he was engaged to Flora Russell, daughter of Lady Arthur
Russell. I have not yet even seen her: but I have no doubts—as
to *her.* (By this I suppose that I alluded to her mother, who has
succeeded in breaking off the engagement, for the time at least.
April 1902.)

At Easter Thoby elected to a scholarship at Trinity.

On 1 April I went with Thoby, Virginia and Adrian to
Pollock's house at Hindhead, my purpose being to help Mrs.
Tyndall about her proposed life of her husband. I had to send

for a doctor, who discovered that I had a complaint requiring surgery. I returned to London and consulted Allingham who advised an operation. Meanwhile George and Vanessa had been to Rome to the Pasolinis, and hearing of my illness returned. George begged me to take another opinion and Sir F. Treves has advised me to put off the operation for some time. It is enough to say now that I consider this to be equivalent to a warning that my journey is coming to an end. How long it will be does not seem to be foreseeable; but not very long, and all down-hill. At present I have only discomfort. We must all make the best of it! 23 April 1902.

Adrian passed his examination for Trinity and his Littlego at Easter 1902. Poor Arthur Fisher died a short time ago. 23 April 1902.

28 June 1902. Dear Thoby's disappointment at dropping into the second class of the Classical tripos has been a trouble but he has taken it bravely. He is off to Freiburg to cram German.

I was made K.C.B. two days ago on occasion of the Coronation—which event has been postponed. I boggled over accepting an honour not, to my mind, appropriate to the literary gent; but gave way to my family who, like other people, would have thought my scruples absurd. My motives for refusing, as Thoby suggested, were not pure—perverted vanity perhaps! Anyhow the thing has been pleasantly received. I am also elected a Vice President of the Royal Historical Society. I have as many honours as I deserve.

28 September 1902. Summer holiday at Fritham again. My illness kept me pretty close to the house, but has not (so far as I can tell) got much worse or better. Thoby with us after the first few days.

George had an offer of a librarianship in the House of Commons from Gully, the Speaker, but preferred to become Private Secretary to Austen Chamberlain who has been appointed Postmaster-General. George most of the time at Fritham; Gerald at Aix again for his rheumatics.

23 January 1903. Adrian went up to Trinity in October and has enjoyed himself! Thoby gone there to cram for civil service examination.

I have had my operation. Went into hospital 11 December; Treves performed next day; returned to Hyde Park Gate on

6 January 1903. The operation successful but started a trouble with the bladder, causing pain and anxiety. The worst day, judging from my own sensations, was 25 December. This trouble gradually diminished and I am now nearly right, I hope. Have not needed Seton's attentions for more than a week, and he hopes to be needless in future. Treves saw me today and speaks well of my state: but I can see that henceforward I must be content to take things easily.

Herbert Fisher died 17 January 1903, aged seventy-six. Heart has long been weak and the cold weather killed him. I envy his quiet end; may mine be like it! He was a man of many fine qualities, kept down by excessive diffidence and perhaps over-anxiety. For the last few years he has been brother-like to me.

Hervey Fisher has been strangely improving.

14 November 1903. Dictated to Virginia.

I shall write no more in this book. I just note that an operation was performed on me by Sir F. Treves on 12 December 1902. It was considered to be successful, and I improved in strength for two or three months afterwards. Since that time, I have been growing weaker, and I fancy that I shall do no more work. We spent the summer at Netherhampton, Salisbury. I am now in bed at 22 Hyde Park Gate. I have only to say to you, my children, that you have all been as good and tender to me as anyone could be during these last months and indeed years. It comforts me to think that you are all so fond of each other that when I am gone you will be the better able to do without me.

*   *   *

Sir Leslie Stephen died on 22 February 1904, at 7.00 a.m.

INDEX